Linking Home and School

Partnership in Practice in Primary Education

Hugh Waller and Jenny Waller

David Fulton Publishers

London

David Fulton Publishers Ltd
Ormond House, 26–27 Boswell Street, London WC1N 3JD

First published in Great Britain by David Fulton Publishers 1998

Note: The right of Hugh Waller and Jenny Waller to be identified as the authors of this work has been asserted by them in accordance with the Copyright, Designs and Patents Act 1998

British Library Cataloguing in Publication Data
A catalogue record for this book is available from the British Library

ISBN 1–85346–482–1

Typeset by FSH, London
Printed in Great Britain by Bell & Bain Ltd, Glasgow

Contents

Foreword

I am delighted to write a foreword to this book.

I have been acquainted with the innovative home–school development work at Moordown St John's School in Bournemouth for a number of years and have always felt inspired and impressed by the school's commitment to actively pursuing partnership with parents.

Hugh, Jenny and their colleagues at the school have initiated a range of imaginative and effective projects that have permeated all areas of the curriculum and school life. The scale and quality of these attest to the fact that close working relations between teachers and parents on behalf of the children they have in common are both achievable and sustainable.

Educational research and practice demonstrate that one of the key indicators of an effective school is an active home–school policy, integral to which is the philosophy that by involving the parents, children's achievement is enhanced.

Hugh and Jenny Waller and their colleagues are sharing their ideas and experience through the medium of this book. I applaud their willingness to provide so many practical examples of 'what works' and to invite the readers to try out and adapt the suggestions and strategies described in the book.

The government is committed to raising educational standards – this book provides an inspiration as to how teachers and parents can form a working alliance towards that end.

Sheila Wolfendale
University of East London

Notes

At the time of publication the government department with responsibility for education is the Department for Education and Employment (DfEE).

This book also makes reference to publications from the DfEE's predecessors – the Department for Education (DFE) and the Department of Education and Science (DES).

Masters for all overhead transparencies (OHTs) and parental booklets appear in A5 format. A photocopier with enlarging facilities will be required to increase each design to A4 size. Permission to reproduce in this way is given to the purchasing institution only.

Additional materials, among them a fuller range of parental booklets, the home study pack and Infant Record of Achievement, are available. For the latest price list and order form, please contact:

Primary Headstart Publications
41 Branksome Hill Road
Bournemouth BH4 9LF
Telephone: 01202 769659
(answerphone during daytime).

Please note there is *no* approval service. Full payment with order.

Acknowledgements

The substance of this book would not have been possible without the active collaboration and support of many people associated with Moordown St John's CE Primary School in Bournemouth over the past decade or so. We remain indebted both to the teaching and support staff and to the governors who have all recognised the importance of promoting worthwhile links with the school's parents.

Several members of the school's personnel deserve special mention – in particular, Pamela Bailey, Anne Dray, Judith Payne and Celia Wells, all of whom have devoted considerable time and energy to compiling parental information literature and assisting in the planning and delivery of pilot educational workshops for parents. We also wish to recognise the efforts of Angela Bence, Peter Byczok, Ceri Edwards-Hawthorne, Joy Forrest, Susie Groves, Jacqui Harding, Michael Lunn, Avis Macdonald, Mary Thomson, Colin Van Schagen and Sybil Wyatt in contributing to this book. Maureen Mills, as a literacy consultant, has been instrumental in creating a successful parent helper training programme, now in its fifth year of existence. To them all we are especially grateful.

Particular thanks go to Martine Grainey, a former parent of this school, whose considerable skill as a graphic artist has been well utilised in designing a large number of the 'visuals' featuring in this publication. Her creative talent in being able to convert scribbled ideas into finished, attractive designs is very gratefully appreciated.

Also deserving specific acknowledgement is Simon Hewitt, a parent of this school, whose photographic skills appear in the samples of parent literature and the record of the school's Learning Support parent workshop. Another is Patrick Sheehan, a former parent of the school, who kindly provided three illustrative designs (OHTs 5.7, 5.16 and 5.18) for the original workshop.

Until local government re-organisation in April 1997, the continued encouragement received from the Dorset Education Authority for this school's many and varied initiatives in promoting parent partnership has been greatly valued. This included a financial grant received during 1995/96 as part of the GEST-funded 'Parent Partnership' awards to schools. The money was used to promote a range of user-friendly parental literature, some of which appears in this book.

Particular mention is made of the following Dorset LEA personnel, past and present, who have been especially supportive – Barry Allsop, Teresa Bain, Ursula Beck, David Bowen, Malcolm Bray, Steve Cleverly, Richard Ely (currently Director of Education, Libraries and Arts), Peter Gedling, Sarah Goddard, Ian Malthouse, David Rees, Harry Turner, Elspeth Wickham, Sue Willcocks and Mike Young.

We have both quoted from and made reference to several publications from the Department for Education and Employment (and its predecessors) and the Office for Standards in Education. Crown copyright is reproduced with the permission of the Controller of The Stationery Office. Other copyright material is reproduced with permission from the following named publishers/ organisations who are the copyright holders:

Bournemouth University
- reproduction of the CCTV parental questionnaire

Cassell PLC
- the 'Wheel' exercise from Wolfendale 1992b (2nd ed.)
- the schedule in Sonia Hinton's chapter in Wolfendale 1989
- the 'parent participation' schedule in Wolfendale 1992b (2nd ed.)

Dorset County Council Education, Libraries and Arts Directorate
- extract from *My Child ... My Story* (Goddard and Waller 1990)
- article about the 'Budget Game' (Cleverly and Waller 1994)
- the illustrative model showing how the Education Welfare Service functions (Bowen 1996)
- School Prospectus Agreement Form (Malthouse 1995)

HarperCollins Publishers/Lyn Wendon
- extracts from *Early Milestones* (Brito and Waller 1992a)

National Union of Teachers
- extracts from their publication *Schools Speak for Themselves* (MacBeath *et al.* 1996)

Open University Press
- extract from the book by Mary Stacey (1991)

Pitman Publishing
- extracts from Crix and Ladbrooke's *School Audit Manual for Primary Schools* (1997).

All other published sources have been appropriately referenced.

This list of acknowledgements would not be complete without paying tribute to our long-standing friendship with Sheila Wolfendale. Over many years she has followed, with great interest, the parent partnership initiatives that have evolved at Moordown St John's. Her invitation to transcribe these developments in a book is a particular honour. We also remain indebted to her for the constructive advice given as the writing unfolded. A similar message of appreciation is extended to John Owens, Editorial Director at David Fulton Publishers, who has assisted us in shaping the book into its present format.

We would also wish to record our appreciation to family, friends and work colleagues for respecting the fact that, for several months, we have had to devote much of our spare time to completing this book.

In conclusion, we trust the deliberate, practical slant of this book will bring renewed impetus to the forging of purposeful and productive links between home and school. After all, it is the pupils who become the beneficiaries!

Hugh Waller
Jenny Waller
February 1998

1 Setting the scene

An overview

The main aim of this book is to offer practical suggestions for strengthening links between home and school. In order to achieve this aim, we need to examine the relationships between the key players – the parents and teachers.

Now that schools are more accountable it is not surprising to find 'partnership with parents' featuring as a key element within the external inspection process overseen by the Office for Standards in Education (OFSTED). Underpinning this is the recognition that effective links between home and school are decisive factors in judging pupils' learning and educational success.

The book focuses on one primary school, Moordown St John's CE Primary School in Bournemouth, of which one of the authors is the head teacher. It charts the development of links between home and school, underpinning examples with research methodology to show how both are inextricably intertwined. While in no way providing a 'blueprint' to be copied wholesale elsewhere, we trust our practice provides pointers for readers to consider within their own institutions.

Why our school?

Moordown St John's was the location for the work developed and described here. The initiatives we shall be outlining are nothing spectacular and are probably mirrored in many schools around the country. The notion of examining this subject from the 'case study' perspective is not a new one, as books by Wolfendale (1989 and 1992a) testify. However, this book offers a deliberate, practical emphasis to complement other works, including those published in this 'Home and School – A Working Alliance' series.

Outlining the book's rationale

Wolfendale (1995) contends that home–school links rest on a number of provable assumptions:

> ... that parents are experts on their own children ... that parental skills and expertise can be constructively utilised in parallel with teachers' knowledge and skills ... that teachers' morale and output is enhanced by parental cooperation ... [and] ... that children benefit from the home–school coalition. (15)

These sentiments are substantiated within the ensuing chapters and the changing profile of this 'partnership' relationship is explored. The White Paper 'Better Schools' (DES 1985) recognised parents as contributors to the education of their children:

> After the child has started school ... parent and school become partners in a shared task for the benefit of the child. The school discharges its part of the task more effectively if it can rely upon the cooperation and support of the parent. (59: 197)

However, as we shall explore in the next chapter, this notion has been widened. The current trend in ensuring a proactive partnership lies in 'empowering' parents. Throughout the book, salient research evidence is offered to substantiate school practice and to underpin the methodology. Implicit in this are the factors that affect home–school relations, including their maintenance and extension.

Much recent educational legislation has had a significant influence on links between home and school. Twenty years ago the Taylor Committee's report (1977) portrayed partnership as a right, in that every parent could:

> expect a school's teachers to recognise his status in the education of his child by the practical arrangements they make to communicate with him and the spirit in which they accept his interest. (43)

Since then successive Education Acts have sought to formalise this partnership. However, as Heale *et al.* (1993) contend, 'legislation cannot bring about an effective partnership' (4.3) – a view we repeatedly stress throughout this book.

Scope of this book

To set our book in context, a situational overview of the school is offered in Chapter 2. In examining the notion of 'parental partnership' from several perspectives, we believe it is a process meriting consideration in any school-based reappraisal of current practice. To this end, in-service activities and resources for use with staff and governors are offered as possible ways forward. The inclusion of 'master' (OHT) sheets enables the reader to create overhead projector transparencies for use within their school or college.

Parental partnership is, by its very nature, an evolving process and the succeeding chapters look at the school's practice from different perspectives. Chapter 3 focuses on ways of strengthening links with home immediately prior to school entry, while Chapter 4 charts the development of a starting-school profile, now available in a published format (Brito and Waller 1992a). Parental partnership in the area of special educational needs is fully explored in Chapter 5. Extensively trialled examples of user-friendly and readable parental guides are introduced in this chapter, along with the complete framework of an activity workshop for parents, staff and governors. Chapter 6 reflects upon the role of parents in providing feedback to assist in reviewing school practice. Using the external audit mechanism, a number of methodological approaches are systematically examined. Again in-service materials are offered, along with some proven practical survey instruments that can easily be applied in the reader's school. Chapter 7 explores ways in which a school's image can be effectively projected through the sharing of curricular and organisational practice. Samples of parental leaflets, along with a workshop example, again feature in this chapter to illustrate the importance of effective communication. In certain instances some of the leaflets can be customised for a particular school, while others can be adapted. The final chapter offers a critical review of recent developments in linking home and school.

Implicit throughout the book is a recognition of the factors governing change and how these have been and are being managed. We would not wish to present the view that all is achieved without discontent and problems.

The *Oxford Large Print Dictionary* (1995) defines 'partnership' as a 'working relationship between two parties towards a mutual goal'. From the educational perspective we find the definition offered by Cunningham and Davis (1985) particularly useful in this context. Partnership, they say, is:

> a relationship in which the professional serves the parents by making appropriate expertise available to them ... it is one of complementary expertise since the expert knowledge of the parent ... complements what the professional has to offer. (150–51)

The transition from preschool to compulsory schooling is one of the most important changes to occur in a child's life, having the potential to make or break the relationship between home and school. It is for this reason that we give it particular emphasis in this book.

2 A closer look at Moordown St John's CE Primary School

An overview

This book portrays an evolving partnership developed between a school and its parent community. By their very nature the initiatives have been developmental. Some, taking the analogy of the parable of the sower, have faded into history, while others have blossomed and flourished.

What Moordown St John's School, a Church of England primary school in Bournemouth, has achieved is nothing monumental. Neither is this book offering a prescription for the one and only way to develop effective home–school links. The success of 'parent partnership' initiatives around the country lies in their richness and diversity, a cause for true celebration. It is hoped that readers will take from this publication the 'seeds' of one or more ideas and, in turn, allow them to germinate and develop into a scheme that is relevant and pertinent to their particular situation and circumstance.

As this book focuses upon a particular school, background information is offered to inform the reader. This then permits a balanced assessment of the initiatives as they are explained in more detail.

School portrait

Moordown St John's is a large church primary school in Bournemouth. It is located within the densely populated residential district of Moordown on the northern outskirts of the town. Since 1 April 1997 it is one of around 40 maintained schools falling under the aegis of the newly created Bournemouth Education Directorate, having previously been part of the Dorset Education Authority.

Originally founded in 1878, it started out providing education for senior girls and infants. Over the years there have been many changes and extensions to the buildings, the latest being a massive re-development in 1994–5. The school currently caters for just over 500 boys and girls of primary age, 4 to 11. The staffing complement is as follows:

- Head teacher
- Deputy head teacher, who is non-class based and has overall responsibility for curriculum management
- 14 other class teachers
- Learning Support department comprising three part-time teachers offering assistance, both in-class and on a group withdrawal basis, in the areas of literacy, mathematics and behaviour
- Classroom support staff numbering six at present, with additional specialist assistants for the Reception Year; added to this there are a few Special Educational Needs support assistants with specifically assigned roles within the school, who are funded by the local education authority
- Administrative staff
- Team of lunchtime supervisory assistants
- Caretaker and cleaning staff.

The school's voluntary aided status allows the Governing Body to appoint the staff. In this way the school governors are able to ensure that all of the staff support the principles of a church school. These are reflected not only in religious education and daily worship but also by applying Christian standards to all aspects of the life and work of the school. There is also a very close association with the parish church of St John's Moordown, providing opportunities for contact with the local Christian community. The school also enjoys close and meaningful links with the residential and business communities in the locality.

A philosophical perspective

For well over a decade Moordown has recognised that its parents should have a clearer understanding of what it is aiming to do for their children and why. Effective communication with parents, as Currie and Bowes (1988) contend, is 'a two way process involving a sharing of ideas' (196). Figure 2.1 illustrates how this may come about.

This philosophy is rooted both in practical experience and in the findings of successive research studies, among them that of Tizard *et al.* (1981). All have demonstrated the positive gains in children's learning when parents are actively involved in the education of their child. Tizard *et al.*'s work offers a clear mandate for schools to work with their parents as partners and to share knowledge and information so as to achieve *mutual understanding* (117–21).

Sharing expertise

Over the years school policy and practice has rightly placed emphasis on parental participation, this acting as a cornerstone on which initiatives have been built. These have focused on the preschool preparation stage, encouraging children's reading, providing support for individual learning needs and developing activity workshops for parents. Known as *sharing expertise*, the process of parental involvement has evolved into one of partnership involving 'a full sharing of knowledge, skills and experience between teacher and parent' (Waller 1992b: 148).

Wolfendale has championed the cause of 'parent partnership' for the past 15 years (Wolfendale 1983). She sees it as being a critical component within the life of schools. In one of her latest books (1997a), she advocates that for 'partnership' to be productive it must 'lead to *empowerment* on the part of parents' (4). This envisages parents exercising full and equal rights and opportunities to participate and power-share – seen as true partnership. While Wolfendale's book is specifically targeted at special educational needs, the concept of 'empowerment' applies universally.

The model of 'parent participation' in Figure 2.2 (p. 6) is adapted from a framework attributable to Wolfendale (1992b: 25). This model tabulates the scope of parental involvement, based on the interaction between home, school and community.

Methodological underpinning

In the sphere of curriculum enhancement, school-focused initiatives have, in part, been influenced by the abundance of research concerning parental involvement. One such example, to which reference is again made in Chapter 7 (p. 89), concerns children's reading, the parameters having been chronicled by Topping and Wolfendale (1985). Among the specific projects clearly influencing Moordown's 'SMART: Home Reading Initiative' (Figure 2.3) has been the Hackney PACT Project (Griffiths and Hamilton, 1984) and the 'Booked by Dorset' scheme evolved by Dorset Education Authority.

In the past decade the value of paired reading as an effective measure in improving both the accuracy and true comprehension of reading among children has been recognised. Morgan (1986) is one of a number of researchers to confirm that children tended to improve in attitudes to reading and that the technique was enjoyable. Morgan and Gavin (1988) express it in these terms:

> It is notable that paired reading allows the child to enjoy the story fully, at the same time as learning to read – avoiding situations in which enjoyment of a 'good read' is denied by frequent halts to struggle over the sounding out of individual words. (201–2)

We have found that, as a technique, parents find it easy to use. It requires minimal professional training and supervision, yet yields a good return in improved performance.

Figure 2.1

Figure 2.3

SHARING IDEAS

TEACHERS / SCHOOL

Explain philosophy underpinning curriculum and method. Recognise and value educational skills possessed by parents.

EXCHANGE INTERACTION DISCUSSION ACTIVITY

PARENTS

Encouraged to use latent educative skills with their children in a way which supports and complements their learning.

OUR SMART HOME READING INITIATIVE

'SMART'

St John's Moordown Are Reading Together

Keys to success

Having already articulated this notion of 'sharing expertise', Moordown's philosophy is rooted in a fundamental belief in child-centred learning. Added strength and permanence is gained by the effective collaboration between teachers and parents. Hinton (1989: 23) speaks of the 'three Cs' (confidence, cooperation and communication) complementing the three Rs. In promoting them as the pillars of Moordown's home–school programme (Figure 2.4, p. 7), we trust that readers will find them evident in the ensuing chapters.

Implicit in the success of parent involvement initiatives is the desire to establish good lines of communication. Moordown invested time and money in developing readable publications targeted at its parents and the children. More recently, funding was augmented by a 'Parent Partnership' grant awarded as part of the 1996/97 Grants for Education Support and Training. The resulting parental leaflets and booklets (examples of which appear in Chapters 5 and 7) can be judged against the criteria identified by Bastiani (1978) – 'clarity, visual appeal, a concern for educational matters and a welcoming tone' (113).

Regular school newsletters also assumed a new style and format (Fig. 2.5, p. 7), composed with care and in a user-friendly, readable style. The school's annual report forms to parents, setting out individual pupils' progress, have been redrawn in consultation with the teaching staff and representatives of the parent body. Figure 2.6 (p. 7) outlines one of the versions, there being four versions in use between the Reception Year and Year 6.

Moordown's endeavours to involve parents of children just about to start school, as part of the preschool preparation programme, echo forcefully the philosophical perspective articulated earlier in this chapter. While this is explored more fully in the next chapter, Figure 2.7 (p. 7) provides an outline of the framework – here the notion of the 'three Cs' can be seen interweaving through these initial, important arenas of exchange.

Links between parents and school continue long beyond the preschool preparation programme and are addressed at both formal and informal levels. At the formal level is the Parents and Friends Association (PFA), which makes a significant financial contribution to the work of the school, as well as holding a number of social and educational events. Speaking of such bodies, Laar (1997) reminds us that 'their greater value [lies] in the expression ... [they represent] ... of communal support for and involvement in the school' (329). There is no doubt

Figure 2.2

OUR SCHOOL'S PARENT PARTICIPATION PROGRAMME

Aspect	Elements	Learning Support implications
PARENTS INTO SCHOOLS	Parent volunteers in classrooms	
	Parental assistance in running library/school shop	
	Parents and others visiting classes	
	Parent-teacher projects (e.g. 'SMART' Home Reading)	*
	Parent-teacher consultations	
	- discussion of progress. review/monitoring of individual education plans	*
	Parents offering practical skills	
	(e.g. carpentry, maintenance and repairs. reprographics, mounting and displaying work)	
	Parents as governors (foundation and elected parent appointments)	
	Fund-raising and support	
	Educational meetings/workshops	*
	Induction meetings - preschool preparation programme	*
LINKING WITH HOME	Home visiting by Head Teacher and other staff	
	- enquiry, fostering relations, imparting information, counselling, discussion of child's progress	*
	Telephone and written link	
	Parent representatives (via PFA Committee)	
	Learning/behaviour management programmes (home/school)	*
	Home-based learning and curriculum follow-up (e.g. 'SMART')	*
	Resource sharing with local community	
	(e.g. use of indoor swimming pool on site/school premises/grounds by outside groups)	
WRITTEN COMMUNICATION	School brochure	*
	Information leaflets. books. etc.	*
	Illustrated booklets for pupils - preparing for school. secondary transfer	
	Frequent newsletters	
	Eye-catching publicity	
	School noticeboards	
	Assessment recording and reporting to parents	*
FORUMS FOR MEETINGS	Parents and Friends Association (PFA)	
	- fund-raising, social. educational and cultural	
	Parent/child induction programme	*
	Educational meetings and activity workshops	
	Links with governors	
	- parent governors, governor 'surgeries', Annual Parents' Meeting	
	Child referral/action/monitoring/review meetings	*
	- case discussions involving staff, parents and child	*
	- multi-disciplinary gatherings	*

Adapted from a framework by Wolfendale (1992b, 2nd. ed.).
Reproduced by kind permission of the author, Sheila Wolfendale, and the publishers, Cassell plc.

Figure 2.4

'SHARING EXPERTISE'
at Moordown St. John's

Confidence
Co-operation
Communication

Figure 2.5

Figure 2.6

OUR SCHOOL
REPORT FORMS
VERSIONS

* Reception Year   * Years 1 and 2 (Key Stage 1)

* Years 3 to 5 (Key Stage 2)

* Year 6 (End of Key Stage 2)

Figure 2.7

OUR SCHOOL'S PRESCHOOL
PREPARATION PROGRAMME
* Introductory Gathering

- emphasis upon the *'informal'*
- school representatives in attendance
- 'circus' of activities: features of preschool preparation programme/ongoing school links highlighted
- start of *'bridge-building process'*

* Resource Support

- home-produced booklets
- video packages (facility being extended)

* School Familiarisation Visits

- weekly 'Collect and Select' sessions
- classroom-based session

* Ongoing Dialogue

- session(s) with head teacher, school-based or, by agreement, in family home
- home visit undertaken by reception teacher

that a school's PFA can significantly enhance the relationship between the school, the parents and the wider community.

Inextricably bound up in the home–school partnership is the Governing Body, accountable to the parents for the education provided and their stewardship of the school – matters on which they report in termly newsletters and their annual report. The pattern of attendance at the annual parents' meeting remains good at Moordown. Furthermore, the foundation and elected parent governors act as channels of communication between the parent community and the Governing Body. Questionnaire surveys are also used from time to time (see Chapter 6).

A comparison of practices in linking home and school represents a natural follow-on from examining the work of one school. While the practice at Moordown is summarised as a discussion 'starter' (OHT 2.1, p. 11), an effective staff and/or governor audit exercise has been devised by Wolfendale (1992b: 30). Entitled the 'Wheel' exercise (OHT 2.2, p. 11), it is a most informative mechanism for representing reality alongside an ideal model of parental partnership. Individual staff and governors can complete this using an agreed pencil colour code and then compare their findings before reaching a consensus. This audit exercise provides a powerful framework for future school-based action planning.

At this stage it would be imprudent not to take account of the ideological and practical constraints that can inhibit home–school collaborative initiatives. Wolfendale (1985a) expresses them in these terms:

- *implications of imposing on parental time and patience*
- *parental involvement leading to diffusion and confusion of role*
- *intrusions upon family life*
- *ongoing parental commitment implications.*

As a consequence of its formal surveying of parental opinion (addressed in Chapter 6) and in other arenas, Moordown has witnessed some of these points from a small minority of parents, yet they cannot be discounted.

Requirements for effective partnership

Implicit in this chapter is the continual message that partnership is a reciprocal process in which there is, according to Wolfendale (1983), 'mutual accountability and mutual gain' (18–19). However, it is important to articulate the notion of 'partnership' from the professionals' perspective. This was attempted by the author in an earlier work:

an understanding of what they can learn from parents about children at home; a respect for parental experience, coupled with a readiness to learn from their knowledge of their charges; an awareness of the parental perception of a child's needs and strengths; and how the parents perceive these needs being best met and their contribution to this joint endeavour. (Waller 1989: 24)

Staff awareness of their potential to block the successful realisation of partnership is important. Caspari (1974) identified appropriate skills and attitudes in these terms:

- *valuing the parental perspective*
- *sharing information*
- *empathising.*

Sensitive use of these approaches to parents results in:

- their readiness to accept other perspectives of their child which are not misconstrued as a questioning of parental behaviour;
- a mutual acknowledgement of the child as a growing person, capable of acquiring skills;
- their realisation that their school has a sympathetic regard for *their* needs (and difficulties)

as well as their child's;
- the securing of active participation in ways that yield success for the child and a new sense of effectiveness in the parents' dealings with their child.

It must be acknowledged that interaction with parents takes time and can only be learned through experience. While Davie (1985) sees this transitional, evolving relationship as being significant in itself, effective work with parents is, according to Cunningham and Davis (1985), dependent on the feelings and attitudes held by teachers about parents. In their research, Solity and Raybould (1988) highlight three fundamental aspects of effective relationship-building:

- respect
- empathy
- genuineness.

To ensure these principles remain at the forefront of the minds of staff, an *aide-memoire* has been devised, based upon each of the letters of the word 'partnership' and printed in a way that can be reproduced as a bookmark (Fig. 2.8). The rationale underpinning this is:

- To remind professionals of their personal attitudes, values, strengths and vulnerabilities and the need for sensitivity to parental needs;
- To help parents to feel accepted and valued as partners, both in identifying a child's needs and in attempting to resolve difficulties through an agreed action plan.

Caspari (1974) identified appropriate skills that have been elaborated and developed to form key elements in Moordown's ongoing staff induction programme (OHT 2.3, p. 12).

Figure 2.8

'PARTNERSHIP BOOKMARK'

To reproduce this, photocopy the quantity required first. Print again on the reverse side making sure the designs are correctly aligned.

Then laminate each sheet, cutting along the lines shown.

Pursue a manner which is genuine
Active listening
Respect
Throw light on assumptions
Non - verbal behaviour (body language)
Establish common goals
Remain silent when there is a pause
Summarise periodically
Help to identify with parents' feelings (empathise)
Involve yourself in what parents are saying
Petition for more information

PROFESSIONALS
PARTNERSHIP
PARENTS

External evaluation

According to Laar (1997),

> partnership with parents is one of the contributory factors that constitute the quality of education provided by a school and is judged on the contribution it makes and the impact it has on the outcomes – the educational standards achieved by pupils at the school. (330)

In looking at how a school is involving parents in their children's education, the OFSTED inspection process seeks to assess the 'systems' in place against objective criteria. We shall return to this important issue of evaluation in the concluding chapter.

Summary

With partnership between school and home increasingly accepted as a decisive factor in children's learning and educational success, Moordown's approach to partnership has been examined from a number of perspectives. We have focused on the value of the parental contribution and parents' responsibilities in developing and sustaining a worthwhile partnership with the school. Correspondingly, we have touched on parents' expectations of the school, both individually and collectively.

There follows a more detailed examination of partnership initiatives developed over the past decade, highlighting both the successes and the disappointments.

THE 'WHEEL' EXERCISE
A Programme of Parental Involvement

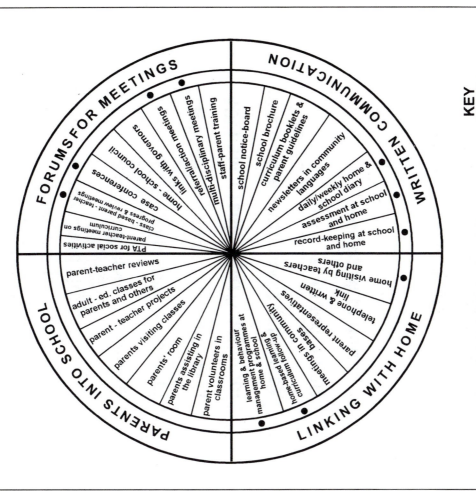

FORUMS FOR MEETINGS
- staff-parent training
- multi-disciplinary meetings
- referral/action meetings
- links with governors
- home - school council
- case conferences
- class - based parent - teacher progress & review meetings
- parent-teacher meetings on curriculum

WRITTEN COMMUNICATION
- school notice-board
- school brochure
- curriculum booklets & parent guidelines
- newsletters in community languages
- daily/weekly home & school diary
- assessment at school and home
- record-keeping at school and home

PARENTS INTO SCHOOL
- PTA for social activities
- parent-teacher reviews
- adult - ed. classes for parents and others
- parent - teacher projects
- parents visiting classes
- parents' room
- parents assisting in the library
- parent volunteers in classrooms

LINKING WITH HOME
- home visiting by teachers and others
- telephone & written link
- parent representatives
- meetings in community bases
- home-based learning & curriculum follow-up
- learning & behaviour at home & management programmes at school

KEY
- ▢ Achieved in last 5 years
- ▢ Happening now
- ▢ (white) Not achieved to date

● : Part of the Special Educational Needs policy and provision

After Wolfendale, S (1992b, 2nd. edn.)
Primary Schools and Special Needs: Policy, Planning and Provision
Publisher: Cassell

'LINKING HOME AND SCHOOL'
'Pointers' for Discussion

* Communication systems
* Information
* Initial contact
  - pre-school preparation programme
* Starting School Profile ('Early Milestones')
* Strengthening pre-school/reception links
* Regular contacts
* Parental support
  - reinforcing classroom programme at home
* Parents as a resource
  - classroom assistants
  - evening training course
* Educational workshops
* Special Educational Needs
  - practice pre- and post-implementation of the 'Code of Practice'
* External Relations Audits

SCHOOL

'LINKING HOME AND SCHOOL'

Principles governing our exchanges with parents

* Sharing information

* Being genuine

* Valuing the parental perspective

* Identifying with others' feelings

* Demonstrating mutual respect

* Listening actively

* Recording salient points

* Summarising periodically and at conclusion of exchange

* Seeking written agreement with substance of notes taken

3 Strengthening preschool links: hand in hand to school

An overview

Some form of induction programme for parents and children in the period immediately prior to school entry has become established practice. Individual approaches vary as pupil-led funding has sharpened schools' awareness of their optimum marketing strategies.

Rationale underpinning our preschool preparation programme

Over the past decade, Moordown's preschool preparation programme has been updated several times. Five maxims now form the basis of our school objectives at the point of entry (OHT 3.1, p. 17), adapted from a framework evolved by Hinton (1989: 24). These could be discussed at a staff meeting or as part of a reappraisal of a school's on-entry programme.

The school's induction programme takes the following form:

- an introductory informal gathering for parents
- resource support:
  - school-produced games
  - video packages explaining the preschool programme and starting-school profile (Brito and Waller 1992a)
- school familiarisation:
  - weekly 'collect and select' sessions
  - classroom-based session
- ongoing dialogue:
  - session with the head teacher
  - home visit undertaken by the reception teacher.

Home–school link packs

Previous research by Brito (1991a) had shown that Moordown's parents appreciated being involved in their child's education and wanted to extend the partnership between home and school. But was it genuine partnership we were working towards, or simply more support from the parents?

The aim was to ease the process of transition into school by improving the relationship between parent, teacher and child. The means of achieving this was a series of enjoyable activities which the partners could share and through which the child could experience success and achievement. The idea was that the activities would engage the expertise of parents who could provide more individual time than a teacher could allow in a normal classroom situation.

The parents wanted their children to do well. They wanted to help but they did not always know how to do so. They were eager to play an active role in their child's preschool development but, at the same time, did not want their involvement to conflict with the school's approach to learning.

A child's education is more likely to be enhanced if all the adults involved are seen to regard each others' views as important. In short, parents and teachers must learn to trust each other.

Wikely (1986) recalled how she and a colleague ran a series of parent/child workshop sessions at a Brixham primary school in 1984. The purpose had been to help parents understand their child's early schooling. She came to the conclusion that parents and teachers rarely spoke the same language, each group making many assumptions about the other in ways that seriously inhibited communication. During the weekly two-hour sessions, the parents and children undertook activities similar to those they would experience in their own classrooms once they had started school. Wikely later interviewed the mothers in order to evaluate the scheme. From the answers she received, it appeared that parents were eager to understand more about the curriculum and modern teaching methods, and would appreciate guidance on how to help their children at home. They were anxious for more contact with their child's teacher, but were wary of asking for it for fear of being labelled 'pushy' or seeming to imply that there were problems when all they wanted was more information. Others would have liked more information about the 'new' curriculum, but feared they would impinge on the teachers' free time. These parents later contributed to the re-assessment of Moordown's preschool approach.

The 'Getting Ready for School' project undertaken at St Mary's RC First School, Guildford (reported by Jowett *et al.* 1991: 169; and in Hinton 1989), outlined an induction programme which aimed to ease transfer into school by enabling parents to prepare their children more effectively. It consisted of a video featuring a typical day in the life of a reception class child. The 'Getting Ready for School' pack was split into five distinct themes, such as time, number and colour. Each section included a relevant story book, a commercially produced game, a cassette pack, a picture to colour and trace, scissors, sticky paper and materials for developing reception class skills. The pack included a 'Let's Remember' sheet for the parent and child to complete, which encouraged the review of activities and provided feedback. The overall response to the project was favourable. The staff felt that it was a useful way of breaking down barriers and that parents had the opportunity of getting to know each other. The children developed a sense of belonging to the school before admission.

'Getting Ready for School' typifies an approach where parental exchange of information and anxieties is a vital part of a behaviour change programme. This initiative came closest to providing a model for the scheme developed at Moordown.

The construction of Moordown's starting-school activity pack

It is at the point of school entry that parents are perhaps most keen to seek advice about how they can help their child at home. It is common for teachers to be asked by parents how they can help, but frequently responses appear in the form of what *not* to do – for example, 'Do not teach capital letters.'

Barrett (1986) suggests that teachers

> give the impression that once you step through the school door there are certain things you don't do as parents and so a lot of natural support ... is taken away because of the school's attitude. (3)

Other suggestions made by teachers tended to state the obvious. For example, 'Share books, play games or visit places of interest'. As many of our parents were already doing all of these, they requested more specific guidance. A structured preschool package, evolved at Moordown and requiring active parental participation, went some way towards satisfying the parental desire for guidance. It offers positive educational support, strengthens and extends the links between home and school and also eases the child's transfer. The games and activities are used at home by parents to build upon the skills and expertise they already possess. This small-scale intervention was undertaken by one of the authors (Brito 1992).

A decision was taken to allocate the summer term of 1991 to the construction of an activity pack which was to become 'At Home With Letterland', although the majority of its activities had no direct link with 'Letterland™', a multi-sensory approach to language drawing upon alphabet characters devised by Lyn Wendon.

The 'At Home With Letterland' package, intended as an extension of the existing preschool programme, was initially used with parents of the reception intake of January 1992. The aim was to encourage parents to present the materials as a stimulus, a series of fun activities for their children during the term prior to school entry. Parents had previously been the children's prime educators and would continue this education but in a more constructive way. They would become more aware of the type of activities which would later be developed in the classroom and of skills which the school considered it desirable for the child to have acquired before starting school. However, these activities were not to be viewed as *homework*. Rather, they would be used to utilise the home as an educative environment and to root classroom-type activities in the children's everyday home experience.

The 'At Home With Letterland' programme consisted of a wide range of stimulating games and activities suitable for children of differing abilities. It was divided into three categories, providing a cross-section of activities under the following headings:

1. *Language and maths games*
   - The inclusion of language-based games was to encourage sound and word recognition.
   - Maths-based games were seen as encouraging recognition of colours and numbers to 10, and promoting one-to-one correspondence.
   - The games were initially devised and produced in black and white format to enable the child, if preferred, to receive a photocopy in order to construct and retain the game.
   - Alternatively, the family were able to borrow a ready-made game for the week.
   - Each game included instructions and a brief rationale as to its educational purpose.
2. *'Make and do' activity sheets*
   - These photocopiable worksheets came in a 'fun bag' accompanied by instructions, a brief rationale and any materials required.
   - Activities ranged from art and craft and cookery to simple science tasks appropriate to everyday life.
3. *'Pick up a pencil'*
   - These consisted of photocopiable worksheets to promote correct letter formation.
   - The 'Letterland™' characters were subdivided into sets of letters containing similar letter shapes, and accompanied by a cassette containing the appropriate 'Letterland™' handwriting verse.
   - Dot-to-dot pictures were also provided to aid pencil control.

Each week, one-hour 'select and collect' sessions were held, at which parent and child were able to visit the school to choose various activities to complete at home.

Resourcing this project was inexpensive, as the originator of 'Letterland™' kindly donated items such as recorded cassettes and videos, in recognition of the school's pioneering initiative. However, we had seriously under-estimated the time commitment required to produce a structured programme of games and activities sufficient to provide 29 parents with the opportunity of selecting three or four activities.

It was interesting to note a change in the children's behaviour over the weeks. Many who were shy and withdrawn initially, and just happy to watch the more confident children taking part, gradually merged in with the others. They were eager and proud to show us activities they had completed at home during the previous week. We decided to provide them with an attractive 'Letterland™' folder in which to file their work. All their efforts were rewarded with a 'Letterland™' sticker.

In fact, a relaxed, well-knit group began to emerge. On average, 12 to 18 parents would regularly attend the sessions. In order to motivate them sufficiently, it was suggested that, in future years, we should provide toys for the younger siblings in a supervised area, and refreshments for the adults.

When considering the criteria for evaluation and assessment of the project, we decided to seek the children's responses to the materials and the parents' suggestions in order to continually adapt and modify them. This led several articulate parents to complain most forcibly about the lack of differentiation. They felt the 'At Home' materials were too basic. This caused a dilemma for us. On the one hand, we were requesting parental responses, while on the other hand, we had not perceived that these responses would conflict with the school's philosophy, especially in the area of mathematics. These parents seemed to be looking for operational competence without understanding, because that had been their own experience of learning.

In the third issue of the *PRIME Newsletter* (1987) it was acknowledged that 'parents ... may have old-fashioned ideas which only value the ability to do pencil and paper calculations. These ideas are easily passed on to children' (1). The *Newsletter* went on to state that '[as] parent anxieties are real, it is thus better to have them out in the open and discuss them' (7).

To alleviate the problem, the reception class teacher later offered two 15-minute sessions at the end of the morning when she displayed the children's work and discussed her methods. However, it must be remembered that the majority of parents were satisfied with both the quality and the selection of games and activities provided.

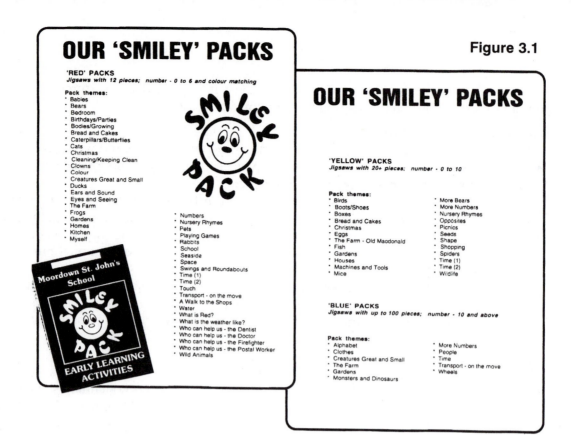

OUR 'SMILEY' PACKS   Figure 3.1

'RED' PACKS
Jigsaws with 12 pieces; number - 0 to 6 and colour matching

Pack themes:
* Babies
* Bears
* Bedroom
* Birthdays/Parties
* Bodies/Growing
* Bread and Cakes
* Caterpillars/Butterflies
* Cats
* Christmas
* Cleaning/Keeping Clean
* Clowns
* Colour
* Creatures Great and Small
* Ducks
* Ears and Sound
* Eyes and Seeing
* The Farm
* Frogs
* Gardens
* Homes
* Kitchen
* Myself

* Numbers
* Nursery Rhymes
* Pets
* Playing Games
* Rabbits
* School
* Seaside
* Space
* Swings and Roundabouts
* Time (1)
* Time (2)
* Touch
* Transport - on the move
* A Walk to the Shops
* Water
* What is Red?
* What is the weather like?
* Who can help us - the Dentist
* Who can help us - the Doctor
* Who can help us - the Firefighter
* Who can help us - the Postal Worker
* Wild Animals

Moordown St. John's School
SMILEY PACK
EARLY LEARNING ACTIVITIES

OUR 'SMILEY' PACKS

'YELLOW' PACKS
Jigsaws with 20+ pieces; number - 0 to 10

Pack themes:
* Birds
* Boots/Shoes
* Boxes
* Bread and Cakes
* Christmas
* Eggs
* The Farm - Old Macdonald
* Fish
* Gardens
* Houses
* Machines and Tools
* Mice

* More Bears
* More Numbers
* Nursery Rhymes
* Opposites
* Picnics
* Seeds
* Shape
* Shopping
* Spiders
* Time (1)
* Time (2)
* Wildlife

'BLUE' PACKS
Jigsaws with up to 100 pieces; number - 10 and above

Pack themes:
* Alphabet
* Clothes
* Creatures Great and Small
* The Farm
* Gardens
* Monsters and Dinosaurs

* More Numbers
* People
* Time
* Transport - on the move
* Wheels

More recent developments

Influenced significantly by ideas contained in Dorset County Council's *Parent and Child Early Learning Pack* (1993), we evolved our own publications, called 'Smiley' packs. Each pack, containing published and home-produced items, is based on a particular theme. Also, each pack provides a source of ideas and activities covering a wide range of skills and concepts. Included within each is a book or books, a language extension or multi-sensory activity, a number task (to 6, 10 or 20), a science activity and a creative/writing skill. However, none is an end in itself; rather, they are seen by parents as 'sparking off ideas' to suit their own child's needs.

Placing these materials alongside the established 'At Home With Letterland' activities, the 'Smiley' packs tend to follow on, being offered to the reception children in the Spring and Summer terms. Given the number of packs currently available – in excess of 50 – they can be offered on weekly loan. The reception teachers have now graded them according to specific criteria, as shown in the current listing of 'Smiley' packs (Fig. 3.1). This enables the staff to match each pack more appropriately to an individual child's needs.

Summary

Although working effectively with parents takes time, energy and commitment, we are left in no doubt as to the advantages. Over the years the teachers have gained a greater knowledge of the child and parental expectations. Similarly, the parents have developed both a feeling of self-worth and a greater understanding of the school's aims and objectives. With appropriate materials and guidance, they have become an effective support to the class teacher.

The positive outcome of these school initiatives is measured not only in educational gains but also in the changing behaviour and attitudes of those involved. As a consequence, there has been a growth in confidence among the parents, reassured that they are teaching in a way that complements the school's approach.

We recognise that parents have a unique bond with their child which no teacher can match. Our preschool preparation programme, with staff offering advice and support, cements the notion of 'parental involvement' at the start. This creates a foundation for continuing involvement as the child progresses through the school.

SCHOOL OBJECTIVES AT POINT OF ENTRY

* Reducing the children's initial difficulties in adjusting to the school routine.

* Offering more information to parents about the challenges and opportunities available for the children.

* Providing parents with the means to play a more active part in preparing their children for school.

* Developing cooperation between teachers and parents in ways that enhance the children's self-adjustment and learning.

* Establishing the foundations for an *effective partnership* between home and school that reflects our 'sharing expertise' policy.

Adapted from a schedule by Hinton (1989, p.24) and reproduced by permission of the publishers, Cassell plc.

4 A starting-school profile at the point of entry

An overview

Assessment at age seven, having now become an established feature of school life, makes it all the more important to have early information about a child's preschool aptitudes and capabilities. It is important to obtain this with the full cooperation and understanding of parents.

For us the notion of a starting-school profile stemmed from work undertaken by Wolfendale (1987). We share the view that such a mechanism enhances communication between home and school, establishing this at the outset of the child's statutory school career. As we state in the preamble to *Early Milestones*, our starting-school profile, 'at this stage of a child's life no hard and fast line should be drawn between learning at home and learning at school.' Therefore, while its user-friendly format does not aim to be more than a first 'snapshot', it aims to provide not only a record of a child's preschool development but also 'a description of the child in the round which is more than a "simple" measurement of his or her abilities' (Brito and Waller 1992a).

Setting the scene

We did not view our starting-school profile as a rigid system of formal assessment linked to the National Curriculum, as this could seem to place intolerable pressure upon the five-year-old child. Rather, we saw the necessity for some form of profile which would assess the needs of the whole child, which would record achievements and provide a 'baseline' for the measurement of progress at Key Stage 1.

Our profile sought to ask pertinent questions which offer an insight into the nature of the child – a holistic view. The unique access that parents have to the home-focused activities and behaviour of their child can only enhance a rounded child profile and complement other assessments. The data from parental involvement programmes, such as Portage, suggest that the quality of the parental input can be commensurate with that of trained professionals. Evidence confirms that untutored parents can abstract salient facts and features about their child in the home context, and report these verbally and in writing.

Parents as educators

During a child's first four years of life, learning is more rapid than at any other time. What is learned at home has a powerful effect upon each child and therefore we must appreciate the contribution made by the parents as educators. It is possible for parents and teachers to play reciprocal roles. Every learning experience at school must build upon previous experiences. The early years curriculum should develop from the child's early knowledge, skills and attitudes built up at home.

Before children come to school they are taught by their parents to acquire language. Most five-year-olds are competent users of spoken language. Undertaking research into early language development, Wells (1987) ascertained that the best single predictor of success in reading after two years in school was the knowledge about literacy the children already possessed on entry to school.

Similarly, Tizard and Hughes (1984), in a study undertaken by the Thomas Coram Research Unit, found that children who entered school with very little knowledge of literacy tended to become those whose reading was poorest on leaving infant school. Therefore, it is essential to make an early diagnosis of each child's reading skills to form a baseline from which to plan extra help for children who are less skilled.

We must not under-estimate the tremendous contribution made by the parents. They are observing their children constantly. They are in a position to pay attention to their behaviour, their moods, their worries, their likes and dislikes, their eating and sleeping habits and their friendships. Before entering school the child will have acquired some knowledge of language and some simple mathematical concepts, and most will have learned a great deal about the wider world. To build upon and develop that knowledge, the reception teacher must endeavour to discover just 'where the child is' and to establish this as a starting point.

Strengthening the link between home and school

The profile can be seen as an opportunity for parents to become more actively involved in observing and recording their child's achievements and in preparing him/her for school.

For the teacher it is a means of getting to know the child before entry, an opportunity for problems and experiences to be discussed and a way of breaking down any potential barriers that may exist between home and school.

The profile booklet acts as a focus for initial involvement. The parents are requested to record their child's development and progress immediately prior to school entry. It is first and foremost a record for the family, and remains their property. However, at the time of its completion it forms a useful basis on which to set an agenda for discussing each child with the reception teacher, social worker or member of another child support agency.

Origins of the *Early Milestones* starting-school profile

We drew upon the work of Wolfendale (1983) who trialled her profile with over 130 children, aged between two and a half and six and a half, from all over the country. It was compiled in the spring of 1984 and trialled over two and a quarter years.

In most cases it was completed by mothers on behalf of or directly with their child. It was intended to be suitable for all children, not only those with specific learning needs. It was trialled in nursery/infant schools, day nurseries, social services day centres and with child psychologists and other professional care agencies. After the original research met with a generally favourable reaction, Wolfendale (1987) used questionnaire returns to create a revised profile called 'All About Me'.

At Moordown we adapted the 'All About Me' profile with the originator's agreement. In November 1989 the *Times Educational Supplement* (Kirkman 1989) ran a feature on how we had piloted this modified version among the 1989/90 reception intake. The article evoked over 1,700 enquiries, many being directed at the profile's originator, and in due course an amended version was published commercially (Wolfendale, 1990).

Her 'All About Me' profile adopted a first-person approach to make it less impersonal. The questions themselves were predominantly open-ended, with the result that assessment of its validity was qualitative rather than quantifiable. The sections of the profile covered seven developmental areas:

- Language
- Playing and learning
- Doing things for myself
- My physical development
- Other people and how I behave
- My health and habits
- My moods and feelings.

Wolfendale's belief is that, once engaged in this type of dialogue, parents are more likely to continue to share concerns and successes with the school.

Our adaptations of 'All About Me'

Our version mirrored Wolfendale's modified schedule although, as an innovation, ours included illustrations as a way of helping parents to complete the responses with their child. In common with its predecessors, Moordown's version explored seven developmental areas, all of which were rephrased for the purposes of clarity, and parents were invited to complete an evaluation questionnaire. The response was overwhelmingly favourable, with some reservations over the format and appropriateness of certain sections.

Although we approved of the philosophy behind 'All About Me', we had some reservations, especially regarding the section entitled 'Beginnings', dealing with the child's babyhood. The school's concerns were later reflected in many of the parental responses to a questionnaire issued in January 1990: 'the "Beginnings" part was hard to remember ... and may be a little irrelevant', and 'I feel that, as a parent, the questions were too open-ended' (Brito 1991b: 2).

The school's version that became *Early Milestones* was designed to be far more useful to the reception teacher, the viewpoint underpinning the questions being that of the classroom teacher rather than that of the educational psychologist.

Early Milestones is not a method of assessment, but a record of information about a child, and is only as full and varied as the information it seeks to present. It values the child's previous experiences and provides a record of development, achievement, progress, concerns and difficulties. One limitation results from the fact that not all parents are totally honest or unbiased in profiling their child. This view came across strongly in an interview with a reception teacher, who reported:

> Nothing compares with actually meeting the child on a one-to-one basis. Some information is quite useful to know (e.g. physical problems, colour recognition, skills with pencil, scissors and crayons). When comparing the information given in the book with the child's actual ability at the point of entry, the two do not always agree! (Brito 1991b: 15)

Many of our teaching colleagues place little value on parental input at this stage, preferring to rely on their own judgement once the children have commenced schooling.

However, Brito's study showed that the profile exercise was worthwhile for the benefit it brings to parents. What came out strongly was the passionate interest of the majority of parents in their child's welfare. Even the less articulate parents shared the same interests. They wanted their children to do well, they wanted to help, but they did not always know how to do so. We discovered the area of home–school liaison to be an area ripe for further development. The parents, this untapped source of strength to the school, were waiting to be involved more fully in the education of their children, if only they could be given the right opportunity and guidance.

Developing *Early Milestones*

The link with Letterland™ Ltd goes back to 1986 when the co-author (J. Waller, née Brito) was given the opportunity to have a set of computer overlays published, which were entitled 'Letterland™ Early Authors'. With a publishing contact already established, we therefore approached them with our initial ideas. Permission being received to illustrate our starting-school profile with the 'Letterland™' characters, *Early Milestones* (Brito and Waller 1992a) was subsequently published.

The rationale behind *Early Milestones* centred on the need for it to be more precise and more pertinent to the needs of the reception teacher. In addition to a complete restructuring of the former profile, the following refinements were made:

- references to preschool experience
- activities to demonstrate the child's degree of hand control, knowledge of colours, ability to sequence pictures, level of vocabulary usage, general knowledge through naming pictures and numeracy skills
- highlighting skills considered useful at entry to school

Figure 4.1

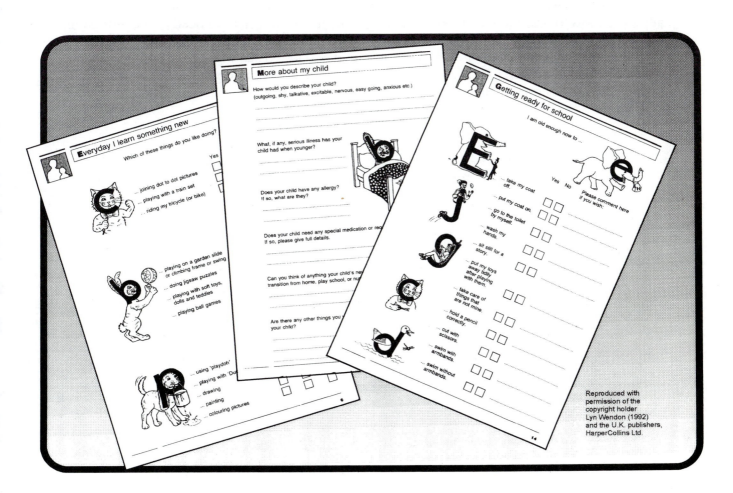

- outlining a framework for parents to offer additional information about their child to ease transfer to school.

Early Milestones appears as a set of photocopiable master sheets that are divided into four sections, each of which reflects the additions listed above – 'Getting to know me and my family', 'Every day I learn something new', 'Getting ready for school' and 'More about my child'. Figure 4.1 (p. 21) provides examples that illustrate the format of our profile booklet. They are reproduced with the permission of Lyn Wendon, of Letterland™ Ltd., and the present publishers, HarperCollins Ltd.

To our parents, *Early Milestones* represented evidence of the school's concern to strengthen the home–school link and to enable parents to offer a valuable contribution to their child's future schooling, as these questionnaire responses imply:

'[It] made ... [my child] feel a part of the school before she joined.'
'[It] also helps the mums to feel more at ease knowing that their child does not start school as a complete stranger.'
'A more valuable means of sharing information ... as things are often forgotten during parent–teacher interviews.' (Brito 1992: 154)

As Brito states in a case study that reviewed the impact of the starting-school profile,

not only does this value the child's previous experience by providing a brief snapshot, but also it highlights their record of development, achievement, progress, concerns and difficulties. (154)

Summary

As the authors of *Early Milestones*, we see its purpose as obtaining a profile and a record of the early developmental stages of a child's growth prior to school entry. It is available as a pack of photocopy masters with a licence enabling the purchasing school to reproduce it. Its flexibility allows schools to adapt and/or modify any page which does not suit the need of the institution.

The 'baseline assessment' programme, introduced in 1997, is explored further in the final chapter. In the meantime, *Early Milestones*, as a tried and tested starting-school profile, provides complementary evidence which can be transcribed on to pre-printed profile grids as part of the initial assessment programme.

5 Contributing to the Special Educational Needs assessment process

An overview

Enshrined in law – firstly Part III of the 1993 Education Act, and then re-affirmed in the 1996 Education Act – is the requirement that schools should have in place effective arrangements for managing children with Special Educational Needs (SEN). Schools must also work closely with parents. This chapter offers 'tried and tested' approaches to encourage effective partnerships with parents.

Suggestions are offered for working with individual parents who have one or more children with SEN. The ideas have whole-school application too. We shall be demonstrating that the involvement of parents can visibly strengthen the collaborative partnership between home and school. As Mallett (1995) suggests:

Respectful, collaborative working relationships are most likely to develop where:

- parents have good access to information about relevant procedures and personnel;
- attitudes are constructive; and
- support is available to enable parents to participate. (7)

First things first

However, before partnership can begin we must look at staff attitudes. Otherwise, whatever is attempted in the way of collaborative initiatives could be seriously jeopardised. OHT 5.1 (p. 38) offers some 'starter' questions which might form the basis of a staff discussion when reviewing school practice relating to the Code of Practice (DFE 1994). Governor involvement would be worthwhile at this stage, especially given their role in overseeing SEN.

The notion of 'meetings with the school'

Meetings play an important part in parents' personal involvement with their child's school. They take place for a myriad reasons – from the trivial through to quite complex exchanges.

In the case of children with SEN, meetings have particular significance for both the parents and the school. However, Mallett (1995) contends that insufficient time and attention, coupled with a less than business-like approach, may dilute their effectiveness. Mallett cites instances such as:

confrontations; feeling outnumbered; suspecting decisions have already been made, or that the discussion started before they arrived, or will continue after they have left; having to be the one who makes contact or arrange meetings; having no-one in school who knows about special needs procedures; not being listened to; staff using hurtful language about their child. (8)

To combat any possibility of concern and lack of trust on the part of parents, we have produced a 'Meetings at our school' leaflet (Booklet 5.1, p. 51) which has been well received. It is a guide *for* parents and *not* one where the tone is cool and charter-like and not conducive to partnership. However, it is also necessary for teachers and head teachers to have regard for a helpful checklist devised by Stacey (1991: 98–9). Since this would form a useful discussion starter at staff meetings it appears as a master sheet (OHT 5.2, p. 38). As Gann (1997) conveniently puts it, 'parents do not just want to be presented with problems ... teachers and parent should work together towards solutions' (158).

Our 'Helping Hand' parental guides

The Code of Practice (1994) outlines a framework of planned assistance for pupils who are identified as needing various levels of learning support. The Department for Education (DFE) produced an illustrated compendium exploring each of the five stages, entitled *Special Educational Needs: a guide for parents* (1994).

Our school does not feel that the DFE booklet is fully accessible to all parents, as there are occasions when one or more of the child's parents or guardians may suffer from similar problems to their child. With this in mind we produced a series of simplified, easily readable leaflets for each of the five stages articulated in the Code of Practice. One of these leaflets is included in this book (Booklet 5.2, p. 52). The remainder may be ordered from Primary Headstart Publications (see 'Notes' section at the front of this book).

Strategies such as reducing the length of sentences and replacing educational terms, unless deemed inappropriate, have been employed in all of the draft leaflets. These, in turn, have been shared with Moordown's parents and with outside educational personnel. Their recommendations have then been incorporated into the final versions appearing here.

During the consultation phase there was unanimous support for personalising the leaflets so that prospective readers could know who the key points of contact were within the school. Space has been left for this to be done when adopting these parental guides for use within your own educational setting.

Also produced is a summary leaflet (Booklet 5.3, p. 53) which highlights the focus for each of the stages. There is also a further leaflet, obtainable as part of the SEN leaflets pack from Primary Headstart Publications, explaining the parental complaints procedure. Whether it be a concern with the school or else with the local education authority, this similarly offers advice in a clear and unambiguous manner.

Parental profiling at the statutory assessment stage

The notion of a written parent statement to complement assessments undertaken by teachers, psychologists and others at school was recommended by Wolfendale almost 15 years ago (Wolfendale 1983). In qualifying the need for this 'parental profile' Wolfendale (1988) saw it:

> as a basis for dialogue, to explore parental and professional perceptions, disparate and shared attitudes and aspirations for a given child. Parents can give unsolicited details and provide a vignette of their child which cannot easily be elicited within a traditional interview situation. (18)

The Fish Report (1985), in endorsing the idea as well as the actuality of providing such guidance and support to parents, commented that '[the] parent profile ... [allows] parents to make a contribution which is seen to be relevant, important and which can be balanced with the professional advice provided' (para. 2.3.19; p. 142). To date this has not been properly acted upon, as Wolfendale again argues (1993a). An OFSTED report entitled *The Implementation of the Code of Practice for Pupils with Special Educational Needs* (1996: 25–7) found that parental interview evidence revealed a diversity of experiences which would suggest there was still not enough consistency within schools in general.

Until the recent advent of parent partnership initiatives among local education authorities, funded centrally from the Grants for Education Support and Training (GEST), it would be reasonable to say that practice nationwide had been both haphazard and inconsistent. OFSTED, in their report (1996: 26), called for a more proactive stance in liaising with parents. A synopsis of the LEA 'Parent Partnership Schemes' (Furze and Conrad 1997) appears in a book edited by Wolfendale (1997a). She has also completed a DfEE-commissioned research study on this same subject (1997b).

However, Moordown has produced several profiles for use at what is now Stage 4 in the Code of Practice, namely the multi-disciplinary assessment process. Adapting guidelines produced by Wolfendale (1985b), which appear in the Code of Practice (1994: 72–3), Goddard and Waller

Figure 5.1

MY CHILD . . . MY STORY

The First Years

General Health   **PRESENT CONCERNS**

Physical Skills

Playing

Self Help

At School

Communication

Behaviour at Home

Relationships

Learning

ACTIVITIES OUTSIDE

Further information about these Parental Profiles is
obtainable from: Pupil and Parent Services, Dorset
Directorate of Education, Libraries and Arts, County
Hall, Colliton Park, Dorchester, Dorset DT1 1XJ

devised *My Child ... My Story* (1990) as several versions targeted at specific age ranges. They are
published and marketed by Dorset County Council Directorate of Education, Libraries and Arts
(Dorset LEA). An outline of the headings appearing in the 'Primary School' version is reproduced
here in Figure 5.1 by kind permission of the Director of Education, Libraries and Arts for Dorset.

Among the factors influencing their format have been:

- The absence of rigid questions and answers or an itemised format, which might inhibit a
creative response from parents, thereby suppressing valuable information.
- Conversely, the guidelines not being so loose as to diminish their value as pointers and in
providing structure.
- The use of language encouraging parents to report their described behaviour in observable
terms, yet also allowing free expression of feelings and impressions about the child.
- An acceptable readability level equating with the eight- to nine-year-old stage in the
construction of the profile and in its various components.
- The deliberate use of a user-friendly writing style which not only values the key role played
by parents but also offers a continuing channel of communication with the involved key
professional.

Recent evidence from Dorset LEA confirms that these profiles are contributing to a significantly
higher level of response from parents at the statutory assessment stage. In 1995/96 alone it is
estimated that between 50 and 60 per cent of the families canvassed at Stage 4 provided a
parental profile. This compares favourably with Goddard's small-scale research undertaking
(1988) when the parental response, without guidance, was only 5 per cent. One reason for this
moderate response is that when a child needs a special school place, discussion with the
parents takes place at an early stage of the assessment by the professional involved. As a
consequence, written parental contributions are not then required.

Educational workshop rationale

The idea of educational workshops for parents is not a new concept – many schools have successfully pioneered this approach – but it is useful at the outset to identify the factors (OHT 5.3, p. 39) that enhance a spirit of cooperation and partnership between home and school, some of which can be empirically validated:

- Active involvement, whereby the learning is matched to the participants' experiences, means that their contributions are valued and respected, and there is a sharing in the realisation of these learning goals.
- Social interaction, in addition to facilitating effective learning, enables common ground to be identified, from which researchers (Ashton 1982, Knowles 1990, Pope 1980) recognise that there is a consequential strengthening of the cooperation and partnership between interested parties.
- As Galloway (1982) has suggested, it is important to offer a flexible programme that is tailored to the participants' 'needs and wants', actively involves them throughout and allows time for informal talk and discussion.
- The parents' educational and management skills develop; these can then be applied, where relevant, to a child's learning (or behavioural) difficulties.
- Through the sharing of experiences with other parents it is possible to enhance participants' confidence, thereby not only reaffirming their competence but also nurturing new skills.
- Relevant information is provided about school policy and practice and the availability of resources at LEA level.

Turning attention to the practical considerations (OHT 5.4, p. 39) surrounding the staging of any parental workshop, the following represent the key components, some of which are similarly underpinned by research evidence:

- *Venue.* Any suggestion that the setting may appear threatening can be set aside, as school premises are familiar places to parents and easily accessible. Whilst they cannot provide an informal, relaxed conference setting, nevertheless tasteful decoration enhanced by displays of pupils' work, coupled with the arrangement of the furniture, can create an air of appropriate informality (Photo 5.1).
- *Seating arrangements.* Research from Duignan and MacPherson (1989) indicates that people learn best when they are actively engaged in their own learning. Therefore group education, allowing experiences to be shared, necessitates the organisation of seating around tables in groups of six to eight (Photo 5.2).
- *Group membership.* Previous experience of organising a Special Educational Needs workshop for parents and professionals (Waller 1989) has confirmed the fact that randomly assigning participants to specific groups at the outset (by means of coloured name lapel badges) ensures a spread of needs, perspectives and shared knowledge within each group.
- *Length of the session.* Cunningham and Davis (1985: 124) consider that two hours is an ideal length, particularly if it includes light refreshment intervals before and during the session.
- *Prior communication.* Circulation of a list of course members prior to the workshop event enables parents to assess their relevance, a view that is endorsed by Cunningham and Davis (1985: 126).
- *Timing.* Scheduling parental workshops in the evening does, according to research by Cunningham and Davis (1985: 124), enable more fathers to attend; however, the needs of single parents have to be borne in mind as they are more likely to experience child-minding problems.

Delivery techniques are equally important (OHT 5.5, p. 40). Retention of flexibility of delivery caters for differing needs as well as satisfying parental expectations negotiated beforehand. Issues to address in formulating the workshop content and style of delivery are:

1. *An 'icebreaker' exercise.* Commencing with a short 'light' activity, according to Berger (1987), encourages interaction and, being so placed, helps to generate a warm, accepting climate that

Photo 5.1

Photo 5.2

Photo 5.3

Photo 5.4

27

allows participants to relax and become more involved with their assigned group.

The first part of the workshop entitled '*First Things First*' poses key questions:

- 'What should the school be doing?'
- 'What should parents be doing?'

This produces plenty of discussion and contribution from the participants with the group scribes being kept busy! (Photo 5.3, p. 27).

2. *Brainstorming.* Research (Parnes and Meadow 1959, Beaucham and Borys 1981) has shown this to be an effective means of producing ideas quickly for subsequent evaluation as well as developing a relaxed atmosphere.

   However, as a technique, there are rules governing its use, namely:

   - all contributions are taken
   - there should be no discussion or criticism of any kind at the time the contribution is given
   - all entries are to be recorded by the scribe, however trivial or repetitive (in fact, frivolous ones can help to lighten the atmosphere and so are valid in that respect)
   - each group is to be encouraged to 'freewheel' in the suggestions that come forward
   - at the conclusion of the activity all group responses are displayed.

3. *Structured wallcharts.* These form valuable visual aids for public display. Generated by each group, these charts illustrate the collective efforts of all the workshop participants. Also, as Long (1983) contends, they demonstrate that these are valued. (Fig. 5.4 p. 30–31).

4. *Interactive approach.* Bringing together a combination of illustrated talks, demonstrations, video extracts (where appropriate) and open discussion is, according to Newton and Tarrant (1992), a proven method of delivery. However, they also stress the need for the presentation to be straightforward, avoiding jargon and excessive lecturing (Photo 5.4, p. 27).

5. *Open discussion.* Capitalising on the opportunity to work in groups, it is imperative that participants are able to air their views and attitudes and listen to the perspectives of others.

6. *The leader's role.* The realisation of any workshop's objectives remains dependent upon the valued contribution of those who are actively involved in the delivery of the session, as their collective efforts serve to create the 'atmosphere of partnership'. The workshop leader must exercise sensitivity and skill in:

   - valuing the contributions from parents
   - ensuring that parental remarks are not overshadowed by a presenter's intervention
   - establishing the parameters for a collective forum between the parents and the professionals, in which purposeful exchanges can be voiced.

7. *Visiting presenters.* Their role is to complement the workshop leader. However, they need to be properly briefed in the way the accompanying notes demonstrate (seen later in Figure 5.5, p.32–3). They too need to:

   - explain their role and the terms used with clarity and the minimum of words
   - reveal themselves as competent and caring
   - provide a feeling of honesty and confidence among parents.

All of the preceding pointers are summarised on master sheets, which can form the basis of planning sessions when discussing the workshop model with parent and governor representatives. Clearly there will be some adjustments according to the subject under consideration. What follows is this school's approach to disseminating information regarding the Code of Practice.

'Working Together' – an activity workshop model

The OFSTED report entitled *The Implementation of the Code of Practice for Pupils with Special Educational Needs* (1996) seriously questions the involvement of parents in staff in-service training sessions on the Code, inferring that, while it is well-intentioned, 'parents ... have found this daunting' (27). Where schools have staged courses or special evenings there has, as the Report suggests, been a poor response from parents.

OHT 5.6 (p. 40) provides an outline of the two-hour evening timetable which is largely modelled on an earlier workshop model (Waller 1989). Whilst it addresses all five stages in the

Figure 5.2   Figure 5.3

What should the school be doing?

What should parents be doing?

Code of Practice, schools may prefer to limit the focus; an alternative outline programme appears later (Fig. 5.8, p. 36). However, whichever timetable model is used, the time duration appears to be endorsed by research evidence (Cunningham and Davis 1985: 124).

The timetable framework includes an ice-breaking group discussion activity entitled 'First things first', followed by question sessions, and information inputs. The initial 'brainstorming' activity is based on two key questions (Figs 5.2 and 5.3), the substance of which is tabulated by a scribe.

To illustrate what can be generated from this collaborative activity Figure 5.4 (p. 30–31) summarises the responses from an audience of 70 people attending the evening workshop in November 1996. Furthermore, as the planning notes (Fig. 5.5, p. 32–3) suggest, the scribes are best drawn from members of staff, along with the visiting presenters.

In common with most evaluation studies involving parents and professionals, the findings from Cunningham and Davis (1985: 128) confirm the fact that everyone gains increased confidence in interacting with their child, as this comment reveals: 'We are taking an interest in our children's education, hoping to avoid the mistakes that were made in our own education' (Waller 1989: 67). The same applies to knowledge and skills. Cunningham and Davis report that 'the majority of parents do gain knowledge and skills particularly in their ability to observe, to understand ... child development and to apply these to their children' (128). By learning to observe and interpret their children's performance, appropriate strategies for development emerge.

An adaptation of this SEN workshop model for parents

Schools may prefer to limit the workshop focus to the school-based 'stages' within the Code of Practice. This was a view that emerged from a small proportion of school families attending the

Figure 5.4 (1)

'WORKING TOGETHER'
in the Management of Special Educational Needs

Responses from the 'First Things First' exercise

Question: 'WHAT SHOULD THE SCHOOL BE DOING?'

1. Early recognition and assessment of need.

2. Consistent policy to be exercised among all the teaching staff.

3. Determine set of standards for each age group.

4. Recognition of parental knowledge about their own child.

5. Parental/teacher liaison
    - exercising good 'listening' skills
    - awareness of pre school experience
    - effective relationships very important
    - constant monitoring and review
    - child involvement and awareness
    - discussing with parents how they may help their child at home
    - being open to ideas/suggestions from parents.

6. Selection of suitable and available materials to meet individual needs and adapt teaching programme as necessary. Where appropriate, draw up and regularly evaluate the child's Individual Education Plan (IEP).

7. Develop greater links with playgroups and nursery schools.

8. Where appropriate, discuss the child's difficulties with the child. Reassure the child (and the parents!).

9. Educate/train parent helpers and AWAs who work in school
    - include specific training with respect to children with particular problems
    - provide an AWA for every class.

10. Liaise and seek support from appropriate outside agencies.

11. Provide information for the LEA.

12. Seek to have smaller classes.

13. Be aware of all children's needs, not just those identified as experiencing particular difficulties.

Figure 5.4 (2)

Question: 'WHAT SHOULD PARENTS BE DOING?'

1. Interaction with their child
   - give time
   - exercise patience
   - support
   - understand
   - listen
   - give praise
   - motivate
   - encourage ('dangling the carrot')

2. Learning experiences
   - reading together
   - pursuing variety of activities (e.g. colouring, drawing, writing, model-making)
   - visits to places of interest (e.g. museums, libraries etc.)
   - encouraging understanding (e.g. money)
   - helping with homework
   - playing games
   - enhancing child's knowledge and understanding of their environment and the wider world
   - encouraging individuality
   - helping make learning fun
   - being prepared to have suitable resources at home to help the child (liaise with teacher about this)
   - being aware of what children can generally be expected to achieve at any particular stage
   - using a common approach to work; use the same terminology/methods as at school; be prepared to re-educate oneself as necessary
   - trying not to have battles over homework.

3. Social activities
   - welcoming friends home
   - encouraging social relationships
   - recreational pursuits (games, sports, etc).

4. Consistency regarding standards
   - discipline
   - manners
   - consideration for others
   - being firm
   - reinforcing standards set by school policy, teachers and systems of pastoral care.

5. Confidence-building (encouraging in everything)
   - help the child to believe it is all right sometimes to get things wrong.

6. Awareness of a child's shortfalls
   - avoid generating a feeling of inadequacy
   - avoid comparisons with other children
   - be careful not to pressurise child
   - maximise reward and minimise failure
   - if a child has a specific problem (e.g. dyslexia, dyspraxia), be prepared to find out about ways of dealing with the problem and seeking information about the problem too.

7. Interaction with the school
   - keep in regular contact with the teacher(s)
   - attend school activities on a regular basis
   - seek help, as necessary, from the school and LEA
   - communicate information (particularly about any changes) to teachers
   - express concerns openly and positively
   - encourage the teachers!!

Figure 5.5 (1)

'WORKING TOGETHER': SEN Workshop for Parents
Planning notes for contributors

Key to letter symbols used:

School personnel: HW (Hugh Waller, Head teacher), PB (Pam Bailey, SEN Coordinator), AD (Anne Dray, Learning Support teacher), DS (David Shute, Maths Support teacher), CEH (Ceri Edwards-Hawthorne, Class teacher), SWy (Sybil Wyatt, SEN Governor)

Visitors: SG (Sarah Goddard, LEA Educational Psychologist), SWi (Sue Willcocks, LEA SEN Education Officer), EW (Elspeth Wickham, LEA Education Welfare Officer).

Estimated timing	Workshop sections	Organisational details
5 minutes	Seating of participants into groups ...followed by introductions	1. Participants to be issued with different coloured badges – these denote the table to which they are to be assigned 2. Each table to have one of the professionals who is playing a key participatory role, and who will act as the group 'scribe'; the remaining scribes are drawn from the teaching staff attending this workshop 3. Brief introduction to each contributor – individuals asked to stand when their name is given; provides focal reference point 4. Programme itinerary displayed as OHT (5.6); already issued to course participants before session (part of final briefing papers)
20 minutes	'First things first'	1. HW outlines context for workshop, showing how attitudes have changed over the years (OHT 5.7) and the fact that many children still have learning needs at some stage in their school life (OHT 5.8) 2. HW introduces 'ice-breaking' activity task 3. Group scribe invites member of group to open sealed envelope 4. Within each envelope is one of two question cards (need to be copied beforehand in sufficient quantities): *either: 'What should the school be doing?' (Fig.5.2) or: 'What should parents be doing?' (Fig. 5.3)* 5. Scribe invites verbal contributions from group membership, writing down all suggestions made on large sheet of paper 6. Final results displayed on large noticeboards around room 7. HW leads plenary session where common trends are identified from each group; two questions asked displayed as OHTs (5.9–5.10) (allow 8 minutes for this latter section)
20 minutes	'What does this school do?'	1. HW introduces 'Code of Practice' (COP) (OHT 5.11); SWy briefly explains role as 'SEN Governor' in overseeing management process (Fig. 5.6; OHT 5.12) 2. CEH introduces 'Stage 1' of COP from class teacher's perspective (OHT 5.13); DS provides Maths perspective 3. HW/CEH distribute school's 'Stage 1 booklet' in 'A Helping Hand' series (Booklet 5.3) (questions to be taken after interval) 4. PB/AD/DS outline 'Stage 2' of COP as our Learning Support teachers (OHT 5.14); outline pupil scenario (Fig. 5.7) 5. PB/AD/DS distribute school's 'Stage 2 booklet' in 'A Helping Hand' series; (questions to be taken after interval) 6. HW raises point that 'meetings between home and school' feature prominently; opportunity for the school to explain its protocol (OHT 5.15) and what should not be the outcome! (OHT 5.16)
20 minutes	Interval	1. Tea/coffee distributed whilst audience have opportunity to engage in informal discussion 2. Contributors to circulate among groups to answer questions/clarify points 3. Group scribes get their group to formulate a question (or point of view) for next session

Figure 5.5 (2)

Estimated timing	Workshop sections	Organisational details
10 minutes	'Your chance to respond'	1. HW invites each group to consider the presentations and to formulate group questions 2. As Chairman, HW invites contributions, in turn, from each group 3. Questions to focus upon first two booklets in 'A Helping Hand' series; also on issues emerging from initial group exercise (others to be deferred) 4. Time allowance for each issue to be properly explored (although within stated time allocation) 5. Any of the contributors to be offered opportunity to reply/make comment
15 minutes	'Other people who help us'	1. HW introduces range of professionals to whom school has access (OHT 5.17) (up to 5 minutes) 2. Individual 5-minute presentations by key people from the above list of agencies: *SG, an Educational Psychologist (OHT 5.18); introduces 'Stage 3' of COP (OHT 5.19) *EW, an Education Welfare Officer (OHT 5.20)
15 minutes	'Where to go from here?'	1. SW, as LEA SEN Education Officer, outlines the Local Education Authority role (OHT 5.21); includes references to 'Stage 4' (OHT 5.22) and 'Stage 5' (OHT 5.23) of COP, the multi-disciplinary assessment process and issuing of statements/notes in lieu (OHT 5.21) (allow 6 minutes) 2. SG outlines LEA's parent partnership project – use of parent volunteers to assist families through the multi-disciplinary assessment procedure (allow 2 minutes)
	'Yet another chance to respond'	1. Distribution of remaining three booklets in 'A Helping Hand' series to audience (Stages 3–5) 2. HW invites each group to consider the later presentations and to formulate group questions 3. As Chairman, HW invites contributions, in turn, from each group 4. Any of the contributors to be offered opportunity to reply/make comment
5 minutes	'How we work together'	1. HW to draw together strands emerging from evening's presentation that serve to underline that responsibility for helping children in need of learning support is three-way – school, parents and LEA 2. Problems may arise – strategies for dealing with them (OHT 5.24) 3. Whatever happens ... a proactive, working partnership represents the way forward (OHT 5.25) 4. Invite written responses from parents about evening's programme and the literature supplied 5. Vote of thanks to all contributors ... and to the audience for their involvement

ADDITIONAL ORGANISATIONAL NOTES
* Coloured name labels (sufficient colours to distinguish school personnel, visiting contributors and parents) to equate with number of groups being hosted
* Sufficient tables and chairs to be arranged in meeting area (groups of 6-8 with clear vision of screen) (Photo 5.1; Photo 5.2)
* Overhead projector and large screen required (Photo 5.4)
* Preparation of question cards (Figs. 5.2 and 5.3); then to be placed in sealed envelopes
* Each table to have supply of large A2 sheets (different colour for each of two questions) (Photo 5.3)
* Writing implements (e.g. large felt pens) to be distributed among each group
* Free-standing boards and fixing pins etc. to display completed response charts
* Make arrangements for refreshments and staffing of this facility before/during session
* Prepare sufficient copies or each of the booklets in the 'A Helping Hand' series so there is one for each workshop participant

Figure 5.6

MANAGING SPECIAL EDUCATIONAL NEEDS

Outlining the Governing Body's role

Overview
* Job as Named Governor for Special Educational Needs
* Working with support of the teachers
* Ensuring that the law, encapsulated within the Code of Practice, is fully observed
* Seeing that the Governing Body, as a whole, has an overview of the provision

Responsibility
* In the words of the TV programme: *'How do we do that?'*
* Extremely fortunate with the calibre of the staff here
* Responsibility, however, rests with the Governing Body and with the Named Governor in particular
* School Governors collectively need to be satisfied that systems are in place within the school to enable children with Special Educational Needs to receive the appropriate help

Sharing information Communication
* Both are very important aspects - between parents and teachers, SEN teachers and the govenors
* A tangible example can be seen in the range of information literature being offered at this workshop

Identification and provision Funding delivery of support within whole school
* Similarly crucial issues in measuring the effectiveness of the school's response
* Outline how the school is addressing these points and aspirations for the future
* Promise of sharing regular reports on school policy and practice in the sphere of special educational needs
* This workshop will hopefully provide a good insight into how this school plans the delivery of support to the pupils here

Figure 5.7

TRACKING A CHILD MOVING BETWEEN STAGES 1 AND 2 AND THEN BACK AGAIN

STORY OUTLINE

Setting the scene
* Outline framework of the story of a real child, whose identity has been changed.
* Child in question - an 8-year-old boy called John.

Class teacher's concerns
* Initial concerns about John's behaviour - aggressive towards other children coupled with negative attitude towards his school work.

Class teacher's actions
* Placement of John on a behaviour plan at Stage 1 but with little success.
* John, although not seriously underachieving, considered to have low self-image and to be unable to complete his school work.
* Formal request for assessment by SEN Coordinator (SENCO), having first been discussed with John's parents.

SEN Coordinator's findings
* Assessment revealed John to be very slightly dyslexic.
* Placement of John at Stage 2 in COP.

Joint action planning
* John received some withdrawal group teaching although due care taken as to how he would perceive this.
* Class teacher and SENCO talked to John about his dyslexia; at first his behaviour deteriorated still further!
* In coming to terms with the situation John's reading and spelling improved significantly.

Review
* Demand for places within SENCO's withdrawal groups meant that numbers constantly reviewed.
* Consensus view that John should leave the withdrawal group.
* Proposal shared with John's parents and with John too!

The way forward
* Retention of John at 'Stage 2' since SENCO still reviewed him.
* Review of John's behaviour by SENCO on monthly basis; no specific teaching at these times, rather focus upon behaviour incidents (if any) that had arisen.
* With John's behaviour modified, attention could now focus upon quality of work - presentation, amount completed within prescribed time.
* Ongoing monitoring of John's reading and spelling performance.
* Given sustained progress over time (e.g. 2 terms), John transferred to Stage 1.
* Eventually SENCO and John's latest class teacher decide if John can leave the SEN Register.
* For other pupils, situation may not be so encouraging; in such cases children move to Stage 3.

Story outline compiled by PAM BAILEY, SEN Coordinator, Moordown St John's CE Primary School, Bournemouth to whom the authors offer grateful acknowledgement.

Figure 5.8

'WORKING TOGETHER'
The 'school-based' stages in managing children with special educational needs

Date:

....

OUR 'ACTIVITY WORKSHOP' TIMETABLE

7.15-7.25pm. Participants arrive
...light refreshments to be served

7.25-7.30pm. Seating of participants into groups
...followed by introductions

7.30-7.50pm. 'First things first'

7.50-8.20pm. 'What does this school do?
* Introduction to the 'Code of Practice'
* Looking at 'Stage 1' and 'Stage 2' of the Code
* Ways of checking the progress of children

8.20-8.55pm. Interval
...time for informal discussion
... 'hands on' opportunities using the resources available
...and more coffee/tea!

8.55-9.05pm. 'Your chance to respond'

9.05-9.20pm. 'Other people who help us
...and how they support 'Stage 3' of the 'Code of Practice'

9.20-9.25pm. 'Any more questions?'

9.25-9.30pm. 'How we work together'

November 1996 workshop, of which this represents a typical response:

> Given that only a very few children go beyond Stage 2 ... it would seem sensible to cut down the time devoted to these later stages ... to allow more time to be spent dealing with the earlier stages ... However, it is quite right to explain the later stages ... but this could be in less detail.

Whilst acknowledging this line of argument, in defending our original workshop model, we had used this to introduce the series of parental guides, to which reference has already been made (p. 24). Since some schools may prefer to offer a restricted itinerary, touching only briefly on Stages 4 and 5, an alternative workshop itinerary has been produced (Fig. 5.8). However, much of the earlier and later inputs remain unaltered.

Other ways forward

Mallett (1995) confirms that a school's SEN policy, presented in a clear and readable format, should be made available to parents:

> Its existence, the thinking that has gone into it and the fact that it will be referred to in annual reports and updated as appropriate all indicate that children with special educational needs are part of the school's agenda. (11)

Although our complete SEN policy, entitled 'Individual Learning Needs' (Bailey *et al.* 1997), is available to any parent upon request, an illustrated summary guide (Booklet 5.4, p. 54) ensures that everyone within the school community is able to see how the values held by the staff and governors are translated into practice. As Mallett asserts, 'parents constitute an important source of feedback on many aspects of SEN policy and practice' (10). Mallett cites examples where parental feedback is worthwhile, such as when arrangements do not appear to be working for a particular child or helpful suggestions are offered to prospective parents.

Another initiative which is gaining momentum is the notion of 'parental support groups'. Moordown offers informal support groups for parents of children with dyslexia, dyspraxia and attention deficit disorder. Supported by key members of the teaching staff, each group focuses upon offering mutual support and encouragement, as well as a means of exchanging 'tried and tested' home management strategies. Our school groups are, in turn, linked to local branch associations, so extending the support network.

Summary

Wolfendale (1995: 15–21) considers that the effects of home–school links within SEN could and should be considerable. She suggests that schools should give serious consideration to the following three issues:

1. The information they provide for parents
2. The ways in which they involve parents in assessment, review and learning
3. The procedures they have for listening and responding to parental concerns and complaints.

Underpinning these requirements is the existence of the Code of Practice. This offers a constant reference to parents who now expect to be informed, consulted and involved at every stage.

The practices that have evolved at Moordown are rooted in a desire to strive for the best for the children. Wolfendale (1995) expresses it in these terms:

> Those of us with a long-standing commitment to active partnership unequivocally endorse the stage that has been reached with parental rights, entitlement and responsibilities set alongside those of schools and the LEA. We owe it to children to work hard on their behalf to ensure that our partnership rhetoric is now matched by substantial high-quality dialogue and negotiation which test parental and professional knowledge, expertise and commitment – and do not find them wanting. (19)

A CHECKLIST FOR TEACHERS IN TALKING WITH PARENTS ABOUT THEIR CHILD

* **Be honest and specific**

* **Be flexible**
  Seek the parents' opinion so that you can work together on solutions and ideas.

* **Observe carefully**
  Notice how you are feeling and how that is affecting the discussion.
  Recognize that parents may be feeling inhibited or tense and give time for them to take in what you are saying and offer their views.

* **Listen**
  Concentrate and show you are listening by adopting an appropriate posture and by seeking clarification, reflecting and summarizing.

* **Help the parents relax**
  They are on your territory.
  Give them a chance to contribute to the conversation.

* **Allow silences for thought and reflection**
  Many of us have been brought up to believe that silences are awkward.
  Yet talking can be an interruption and disruptive.
  Silences allow people time to collect their thoughts and continue.

* **Be positive about the child**
  Give examples, not generalities.

* **Ask questions which lead the conversation**
  Avoid putting answers in the parents' mouth.
  Allow questions which are difficult or challenging for you.

* **Answer questions honestly**
  Avoid justifying or going on the defence.
  If it is difficult for you to say, express a feeling.
  If you do not know the answer then admit this.
  Do not make promises which you know you cannot fulfil or reassure with improbabilities.

* **Remember, good relationships take time**
  Allow the relationship to grow.
  It is not friendship, but a viable working partnership that you are seeking.
  This does not mean that you have to agree on everything but it means you need to respect and value each other's experience.

Extract taken from Mary Stacey's book: *Parents and Teachers Together* (1991) and reproduced by kind permission of the publisher, Open University Press (98-9).

FIRST THINGS FIRST
Seeking staff consensus about home-school link initiative

* Does everyone fully understand the proposition being considered? If not, make this clear at the outset.

* What are the resource implications - human and material?

* How is the project to be managed and what systems are in place to monitor and evaluate its effectiveness?

* Is the proposal in keeping with the current ethos and values displayed by our school?

* Does the initiative accord with the parental perspective about linking home and school?

* Is everyone committed to translating this proposal into practice ... and, in so doing, strengthening the home-school partnership through its success?

EDUCATIONAL WORKSHOPS
Practical considerations

* Choose venue with sufficient space for expected audience

* Arrange seating into groups with 6-8 people each around a table

* Distribute audience fairly (staff, governors, parents and visitors) - use pre-printed coloured name badges

* Keep workshop to a maximum two-hour length

* Circulate participants with sufficient information beforehand

* Choose evening slot for parent workshops

EDUCATIONAL WORKSHOPS
Keys to success

* Canvass audience beforehand
  - workshop then appropriately targeted

* Pitch learning and management techniques to needs of audience

* Provide opportunities for 'sharing' ideas
  - a confidence-builder!

* Give everyone 'ownership' of event by letting them socialise during proceedings

* Build flexibility into programme

* Use variety of teaching approaches
  - get everyone participating from outset
  - have several discussion 'spots'
  - keep inputs from visiting speakers brief
  - intersperse with audio visual aids (OHPs, video)

* Intersperse with relevant information about school policy and practice

'WORKING TOGETHER'
in managing children with special educational needs

Date:

....

OUR 'ACTIVITY WORKSHOP' TIMETABLE

7.15-7.25pm. Participants arrive
              ...light refreshments to be served

7.25-7.30pm. Seating of participants into groups
              ...followed by introductions

7.30-7.50pm. 'First things first'

7.50-8.10pm. 'What does this school do?'
              * Introducing the Code of Practice
              * Looking at Stage 1 and Stage 2 of the Code

8.10-8.30pm. Interval
              ...time for informal discussion...and more coffee/tea!

8.30-8.40pm. 'Your chance to respond'

8.40-8.55pm. 'Other people who help us'
              * 'Just how many are there?'
              * The Educational Psychologist
              * The Education Welfare Officer

8.55-9.10pm. 'Where do we go from here?'
              * The role of the Local Education Authority
              * The Authority's 'Parent Partnership' Project

9.10-9.25pm. 'Yet another chance to respond'
              * Looking at our 'Helping Hand' leaflets (Stages 3 to 5)
              * Any questions?

9.25-9.30pm. 'How we work together'

EDUCATIONAL WORKSHOPS
Teaching strategies

* Begin with activity that gets audience fully involved

* Generate ideas from audience through 'brainstorming' technique

* Provide opportunities for 'valuing' group efforts by displaying wallcharts

* Include range of information-delivery strategies:
   - illustrated talks
   - demonstrations
   - video extracts (*where appropriate*)
   - open discussion

* Be clear about your role as workshop leader

* Offer clear briefing instructions to visiting speakers well beforehand

* Ensure everyone involved is clear about every facet of educational workshop

Many children will have learning needs at some stage

It's not like this now ... thankfully!

What should parents be doing?

What should school be doing?

MANAGING SPECIAL EDUCATIONAL NEEDS

Our Governing Body's role

* Overview

* Responsibility

* Sharing information

* Communication

* Identification and provision

* Funding delivery of support within whole school

'STAGES' IN THE CODE OF PRACTICE

'STAGE 1'
* Initial identification of concern
* Entry of child's name on school's 'Special Educational Needs Register'
* Discussion with parents
* Monitoring by child's class teacher

'STAGE 2'
* Continuing concerns after monitoring
* More discussion with child's parents
* Gathering of information by one or more of school's Learning Support teachers (usually the Special Educational Needs (SEN) Co-ordinator)
* Drafting of special teaching programme for the child known as an 'Individual Education Plan' (IEP), to progress the learning
* IEP actioned by child's teacher(s)
* Regular reviews

'STAGE 3'
* Increasing concerns about child's progress
* SEN Co-ordinator seeks specialist advice from professionals (e.g. educational psychologist, a specialist teacher, a speech and language therapist, or someone else from the support services)
* Regular reviews with child's parents

'STAGE 4'
* Decision to ask Local Education Authority (LEA) to consider whether a statutory assessment is appropriate (usually done by headteacher)
* Statutory assessment is started, if LEA considers it appropriate
* Advice collected by an Education Officer

'STAGE 5'
* LEA considers advice collected
* Decision taken whether a 'Statement of Special Educational Needs' should be made
* If 'Yes' then Statement prepared with arrangements to monitor and review child's progress
* If 'No' then detailed report (known as a 'note in lieu') prepared setting out LEA reasons for not making a Statement

'A HELPING HAND'
Stage 2

* What has happened so far?

* Seeking more support

* What happens now at 'Stage 2'?

* Reviewing your child's progress

'A HELPING HAND'
Stage 1

* Introduction

* What is the 'Code of Practice'?

* Working step-by-step

* What happens at 'Stage 1'?

* Reviewing your child's progress

* If more needs to be done

It's not the outcome we're seeking!

MEETINGS AT OUR SCHOOL

* Meet for a purpose

* Meet without delay

* Agree best time

* Allow sufficient time for exchange

* Respect privacy

* Be prepared

* Offer right setting

* Everyone given a 'say'

* Consider issues carefully and thoroughly

* Receive record of meeting

* Confidential information respected

* Ask questions . . . at every stage

* Agree next meeting date . . . if required

An Educational Psychologist...?

THOSE WHO ARE THERE TO HELP US...

From the Local Education Authority:

* Learning Support Service
* Educational Psychologist
* Behaviour Support Service
* English as an additional language
* Education Welfare Officer
* Audiologist and Hearing Impaired Service
* Education Officers and support staff

From the medical services:

* Community Paediatrician
* School Nurse
* Speech and Language Therapist
* Physiotherapist
* Occupational Therapist
* Child and Family Guidance

...and other health specialists

From other agencies:

* Social Worker

...and possibly others too

Education Welfare Service tries to address the needs of the individual

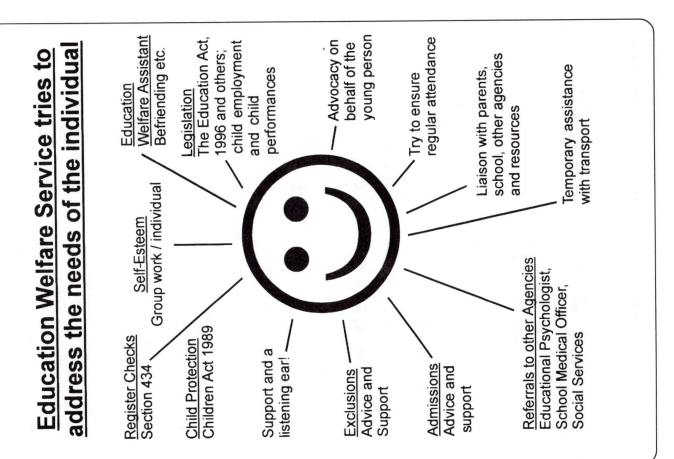

Register Checks
Section 434

Self-Esteem
Group work / individual

Education Welfare Assistant
Befriending etc.

Legislation
The Education Act, 1996 and others; child employment and child performances

Child Protection
Children Act 1989

Support and a listening ear!

Advocacy on behalf of the young person

Try to ensure regular attendance

Liaison with parents, school, other agencies and resources

Temporary assistance with transport

Exclusions
Advice and Support

Admissions
Advice and support

Referrals to other Agencies
Educational Psychologist, School Medical Officer, Social Services

---

'A HELPING HAND'
Stage 3

*   **What has happened so far?**

*   **Seeking further help**

*   **What else happens at 'Stage 3'?**

*   **Reviewing your child's progress**

'A HELPING HAND'
Stage 4

* What has happened so far?

* What is a 'statutory assessment'?

* The stage reached by my child

* What the Local Education Authority is doing

* Who is a 'Named Person'?

* Help is at hand

* Having your say

* How long do we wait for the LEA's decision?

* What happens if there is to be no assessment?

* If the assessment proceeds . . . .

* Different types of special help available

* You and your child during the assessment process

* Making your contribution

* Getting independent advice

* What are the outcomes?

* Have we answered all of your questions?

* If not, do ask again

THE TIMING OF THE ASSESSMENT PROCESS

Request for a 'Statutory Assessment' from a school and/or a child's parents

6 weeks — Local Education Authority considers whether or not to undertake a 'Statutory Assessment'

DECISION → not to assess

to assess

10 weeks — LEA seeks advice from the child's parents and all professionals concerned (6 weeks allowed)

DECISION → not to make a Statement

DECISION to make a Statement

Proposed Statement

notice, with full reasons (preferably in the form of a 'Note in lieu')

8 weeks

Final Statement

Total = 26 weeks

Adapted from a chart appearing in the Department for Education's 'Code of Practice on the Identification and Assessment of Special Educational Needs' publication (1994), 51.

Crown copyright is reproduced with the permission of the Controller of The Stationery Office.

48

STILL UNHAPPY?
WHAT TO DO NEXT . . .
A Parental Complaint Guide

* Are you dissatisfied with this school's handling of your child? If so, please read on

* Sometimes it is a matter of misunderstanding . . .

* There's help at hand

* What if you still disagree with this school?

* Disagreeing with the Local Education Authority

'A HELPING HAND'
Stage 5

* What has happened so far?

* What is a 'Statement'?

* With the Statement completed, what happens next?

* You need to respond quickly

* Completing the final Statement

* With the Statement in place, what happens next?

* Annual review of the Statement

* Have we answered all of your questions? If not, do ask again

Our maxim:
'Working together' in the best interests of the child

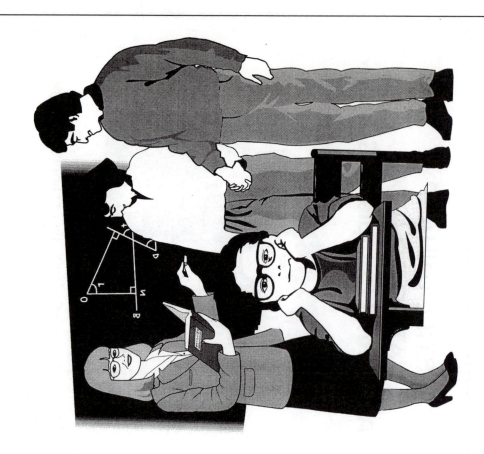

Keeping a record of the meeting
So that we remember all that has been said we take notes of our discussion together. From this information we can then all agree the target(s) we want to set to help your child make progress. This we call an 'individual education plan' (IEP).

We shall be pleased to let you have a copy of the notes we take and the IEP as well. It may be that part of this plan will include you helping your child at home to reach one or more of the targets we have all agreed.

It is also helpful to us all if we fix a date when the next meeting needs to take place, if this is what we all want.

Respecting confidentiality
Sometimes we may need to get information from your doctor or other health service workers. We are grateful when you agree to this as we can always offer the best help when we are well informed.

The information we share at a meeting is always treated very carefully. We do <u>not</u> pass on information about your child without your permission. Records are kept locked away when they are not in use.

Any other points?
If there is anything you are not sure of ... *before, during and after the meeting* ... we hope you will feel at ease to ask.

If we are to work together in your child's best interests then we <u>all</u> need to be clear about what is happening.

MEETINGS AT OUR SCHOOL

Place your school logo here

Why do we need to meet?
There will be times when you need to talk to the head teacher or your child's teacher about a concern. It could be that we would like to see you.

Our meetings are for different reasons. It could be a difficulty in learning or behaviour . . . or a medical concern . . . or even a family matter that needs to be shared.

We are sure you will agree it is important for us to meet at the earliest opportunity as we want to be of help to you. We would like you to make an appointment first.

Choosing the right time for the meeting
At all times we wish to be helpful and flexible about when and where we should meet. Mostly our meetings are held at our school in a room where we are not going to be disturbed.

Our meetings are usually:
* ....
*or ....
These are hopefully acceptable times that suit you. We can then have time to listen to each other, hopefully easing the problem .... and resolving it.

The best ways to contact us at school
If you have any concerns about your child we would like to know so we can talk together and see what can be done. You can tell us by:
* *writing a note to your child's teacher or head teacher*
* *telephoning at breaktime or lunchtime*
* *commenting briefly to the teacher after the class has been dismissed at the end of the session.*
We shall then arrange a meeting as soon as is convenient to all of us.

Being prepared for the Meeting
Before we meet it is important that we all know why it is taking place. With more formal meetings we always share the agenda with you beforehand. You will also be sent copies of any reports we would like to talk about when we meet.

Those attending the meeting
We will always try to ensure you are told who else will be attending the meeting we have arranged, and the job they have. Please be assured that anyone who attends will be there to help you and your child.

We will also be happy for you to bring someone along, who will be made very welcome by us.

Having the right setting for the meeting
We would like you to feel 'at home' and comfortable when we all meet. Some of you may prefer it if we sit around a table, especially if there are papers to study. This we can agree upon when we meet together.

What we do at the meeting
At our meeting, time is given so that we can all share information and views. We are especially eager to hear what <u>you</u> wish to say about your child. We may want to show you examples of work your child has done.

It is important for us all to look carefully and thoroughly at what the concerns are, and to be honest with one another. It may be we shall be saying things like:
'. . . What I have tried has not worked very well so I think I should. . .'

STAGE
3

A HELPING HAND

A Guide for Parents with children at Stage 3
of the Code of Practice for children with
Special Educational Needs

YOUR
SCHOOL
LOGO
HERE

What has happened so far

Your child may have been given help at Stage 2. You and all your child's other teachers, including our school's Special Educational Needs (SEN) teaching staff:

....

will have talked together and agreed what needs to be done now.

Seeking further help

This is called 'Stage 3'. There are many people outside our school who can now help. They are called 'specialist' help. It might be an educational psychologist, or a specialist teacher, or someone from the support services. We will tell you what they can do.

What else happens at 'Stage 3'

Your child's SEN teacher will look at all he/she knows about your child, asking:
'What has been done so far?' and
'What do we need to do now to help your child?'

All the teachers and the specialist(s) will then decide on an 'individual education plan' (IEP) for your child.

We want you to know that this school will keep a close watch on how your child is doing. We will keep a record of their progress. We will always try to tell you what is happening. We will invite you to meetings to see how things are going. This is called a 'review'.

Reviewing your child's progress

It may be decided that your child is doing well and does not need the extra help. Your child will then return to Stage 2. But we will still make sure your child is doing well by regular reviews.

If your child does continue to have help from one or more outside specialists then your child will remain at Stage 3. We will get their help in drawing up the individual education plan (IEP) for your child.

If, however, the outside specialist(s) and this school feel your child is not making as much progress as we would like, we may suggest your child moves to 'Stage 4'.

This is when our school's head teacher .... will consider whether or not this school will ask the local education authority (LEA) to begin a more detailed assessment of your child. This decision will only be taken after talking about it very carefully with you.

Leaflet written by:
PAM BAILEY, ANNE DRAY and HUGH WALLER
Moordown St John's CE Primary School, Bournemouth.

The authors acknowledge the grant received from Dorset County Council Education Department to fund the original production and printing costs.

Help in redrafting the text has been given by URSULA BECK, SARAH GODDARD, SUE WILLCOCKS and SYBIL WYATT, to whom the authors are most grateful.

PARENT PARTNERSHIP

Booklet 5.3

'Stage 4'
* Together we ask the Local Education Authority (LEA) to agree to gather information about your child. Your child's needs are such that this request is put in writing by the head teacher.
* If the LEA agrees with us then a very detailed examination of your child's special educational needs will start. This is called a 'statutory assessment'.
* To begin, it must have your permission.
* The assessment of your child will involve several people, so making it a 'multi-disciplinary assessment'.
* You will contribute too.
* All of the information is collected by an Education Officer.

'Stage 5'
* The Local Education Authority (LEA) looks at all of the advice.
* The LEA decides whether it will issue a document setting out your child's special educational needs.
* If 'Yes' then a 'Statement of Special Educational Needs' is made. It will say what arrangements are being made to watch how your child is doing. There will also be a detailed review at least once each year.
* If 'No' then a detailed report is given to you and this school saying why the LEA is not making a Statement.

Some final points . . .

Each of the five 'A Helping Hand' leaflets tells you more. You will be given the one telling you the 'stage' where we have placed your child.

You can, if you wish, request an assessment for your child. However, we would want to discuss this with you first.

If you are unhappy about what this school (or the LEA) is planning for your child then you can complain. What you do is explained in another leaflet. We hope this will not happen as we want to give the right help for your child who has special educational needs.

Leaflet written by:
PAM BAILEY, ANNE DRAY and HUGH WALLER
Moordown St John's CE Primary School, Bournemouth.

The authors acknowledge the grant received from Dorset County Council Education Department to fund the original production and printing costs.

Help in redrafting the text has been given by URSULA BECK, SARAH GODDARD, SUE WILLCOCKS and SYBIL WYATT, to whom the authors are most grateful.

PARENT PARTNERSHIP

Introductory Leaflet

A HELPING HAND
An introductory Parental Guide for Children with Special Education Needs

YOUR
SCHOOL
LOGO
HERE

Introducing our 'A Helping Hand' leaflets

We have written these leaflets to tell you how this school is helping children who have 'special educational needs'. This is called 'SEN' for short.

Our school leaflets (there are seven including this one) tell you very clearly how this school and you can work well together. We all want to help your child who has special educational needs.

The 'Code of Practice'
The Department for Education and Employment (DfEE) has written a guide called the 'Code of Practice'. It tells us about the help we and the Local Education Authority (LEA) should give a child with special educational needs.

What the 'Code of Practice' is
We need to give your child help in the best way. The Code of Practice looks at levels of help. Each level is called a 'stage'. The help your child needs may change when getting older. He/she may need more or less help.
Five of our 'A Helping Hand' leaflets look closely at each of the stages. However this leaflet tells you in a few words about each one.

'Stage 1'
* Looking at the initial concern about your child.
* Talking about this concern with you.
* Putting your child's name on our 'Special Educational Needs Register' *(a confidential record which lists all of the children at our school who have special educational needs)*.
* Your child's teacher watches closely how your child is doing and may set up a special programme for him/her.

'Stage 2'
* We all still have concerns about your child and feel more help is needed.
* We continue to talk with you about these concerns.
* One or more of our Learning Support teachers gather information about your child.
* A teaching programme, called an 'Individual Education Plan' (IEP), is made for your child.
* Your child's teachers use this IEP to help your child.
* Teachers at our school continue to watch how your child is doing.

'Stage 3'
* Ours and your concerns about your child are still there.
* We all agree to look for advice from outside our school.
* Our school's Special Educational Needs (SEN) Co-ordinator asks for help from other people, called 'specialists'.
* These people might be an educational psychologist, a specialist teacher, a speech and language therapist, or someone else from the support services.
* Meetings between you and this school continue. Each is called a 'review'.

REMEMBER . . . only a small number of children go beyond 'Stage 3' - at present we only have .... children out of ....

Our Governing Body keeps a watching brief too . . .

* What this school does in the area of Special Education Needs (SEN) is of interest to our School Governors.

* One of them is given the title, 'SEN Governor'. This person is currently

  ....
  You can contact her via Reception.

* Her job is to:
  - *look at what this school is providing;*
  - *check all systems are in place and working in the best interests of the children;*
  - *make sure this school is sharing information effectively and working closely with the parents; and*
  - *ensure this school is offering good value given the resources available.*

Let us have your views, please

* We really value and welcome comment about what we are offering your child. This includes criticism ... saying it constructively is better!

* If we can do something ... then we will!

* If something concerns you, do tell us immediately - preferably by meeting face-to-face. If you contact us by letter or telephone then we try to respond quickly.

It's all in our 'Individual Learning Needs' policy . . .

* Having consulted all of the teaching staff, the school governors and the Local Education Authority we have produced our written policy.

* Whilst it is available, at cost, from our School Office we hope this leaflet offers you a helpful summary.

* Our policy is regularly reviewed by key members of our teaching staff, the last time being in ....

The following teaching staff are 'on call' to help you . . . in addition to your child's teacher

© 1997 Moordown St. John's CE Primary School, Bournemouth.

Place your school logo here

OUR LEARNING SUPPORT PROGRAMME

'Special Educational Needs' - what does this mean?

* We use these words when we find a child in our school who is having difficulties.

* It may be due to behaviour ... or something to do with being unable to learn easily or quickly ... or even a medical concern. However, it can sometimes be more than one of these.

Being on the 'look out' for these difficulties

* Our school's staff are trained to notice any concerns about a child early on.

* It is usually the class teacher who raises the concern ... but it can also be a parent; this we welcome.

* As soon as any concern is identified we <u>always</u> share this with the child's parents.

What we do next . . .

* As soon as a concern is noticed, we place the child on the correct 'stage' in the Code of Practice.

* All of what we do to support a child (and his or her parents) is explained in a series of helpful, easy to read, parental leaflets - we call them: 'A HELPING HAND'.

A HELPING HAND
An Introductory Parental Guide for Children with Special Education Needs

Place your school logo here

* In addition to giving out an introductory leaflet *(which we will have already issued)* we also provide a child's parents with another leaflet. This tells parents about the stage on which their son or daughter has been placed.

* We hope that our written leaflets and our willingness to answer <u>every</u> question show we are eager to help.

Our maxim: 'Working Together'

* We are committed to 'working together' with our school's parents in every aspect of our Special Educational Needs work.

* We do this one or more of the following ways:
  - *through face-to-face meetings;*
  - *providing for our parents easy to read leaflet guides;*
  - *offering information workshops at which we share our school practice;*
  - *putting parents in contact with other people outside our school, as well as support agencies and contact groups.*

* We hold regular review meetings with parents (and usually the child, too). Here we look at what has happened since our last meeting and agree what to do next. We also decide the date of any future meeting.

* At every stage we are happy to answer parental questions. We wish to share what we are doing to support a child in their learning.

* Remember to look at our 'Learning Support Noticeboard' ....(location) It tells you about the events taking place here and elsewhere locally.

6 Parental feedback as a catalyst for change

An overview

In this age of 'accountability' schools need workable mechanisms to assess the extent to which they are being seen as successful. They need to devise ways of promoting their attributes in a more assertive manner.

Already, educational institutions are exposed to the phenomenon of external audit. This is either through the process of school self-review or else initiated by outside bodies like OFSTED. In both instances parents are called upon to contribute evidence as part of the overall assessment process.

In this chapter we offer you some examples of the external relations audit approach. All have taken the school forward in development planning terms.

Setting the scene

For many years at Moordown we have felt strongly that consulting parents is important, a view echoed by Davies (1988) who states that 'consulting the clients is an important aspect of public relations' (35).

Already, school-generated initiatives in liaising with parents have attracted interest both in the media (Kirkman 1989, Waller 1992a) and in academic books and journals (Waller 1992b, Waller 1993b, Waller 1993c, Waller 1996). Parental feedback was similarly instrumental in helping us finalise the 'Early Milestones' profile at the point of school entry (Brito and Waller 1992a).

Around five years ago, with the reality of a massive programme of school rebuilding becoming increasingly imminent, the consensus view among staff and governors was that we needed to promote our school and its attributes more assertively. This was especially the case given that, as we are a voluntary aided school, parents would need to be approached to assist in raising a significant proportion of the overall building improvement costs. At that time, our Parents and Friends Association (PFA) had expressed an unwillingness to direct more than 10 per cent of its fund-raising to the rebuilding fund, a state of affairs that has since, thankfully, been overturned.

We were therefore keen to identify ways in which we could convince the parent body and, in turn, the wider community, that there was a real need to raise the sum of £133,000. The first of our 'external relations audits' provided an excellent opportunity for this.

Methodological approaches

Given the focus upon the external audit approach in gathering information, Gray (1991) contends that

> the marketing audit seeks to understand the current situation with respect to the organisation's marketing by examining in a structured way all available and relevant information. (54)

With the current emphasis within education upon 'success indicators', a factor to which we shall be returning later in this book (Chapter 8, p. 112), it offers quantitative and qualitative measures for judging the performance of an institution.

The main thrust of this chapter looks at strategies and techniques for seeking the opinions of parents. However, it will not escape the reader's attention that the methods can also be selectively employed among a specific target group within a school community. Information has been presented within this section as master sheets suitable for conversion to overhead projector transparencies (OHTs) to assist a school staff and its governors to become an *even more effective listening institution*. However, the guiding messages are the need to:

• Be clear as to the purpose(s) of the survey.

- Choose the right time.
- Select the most appropriate survey method(s).
- Design the survey carefully.
- Use representatives from your survey audience to help design the survey.
- Selectively test and retest before embarking upon the main survey.
- Be aware that the respondents might not wish to give an open assessment.
- Consider carefully whether the respondents' assessment can be taken at face value, especially if the survey question is too generalised.

Having regard for the range of methodological approaches, the following, either individually selected or pursued as a combination, are appropriate to an education setting, with time and cost implications being governing factors:

- Focus group meeting
- Text-based questionnaire
- Face-to-face interview.

Clarity of purpose from the outset will ensure selection of the most appropriate survey method. Crix and Ladbrooke (1997: 3–4) offer instructive analyses of the 'quantitative' and 'qualitative' survey approaches. Adaptations of their work appear as OHTs 6.1 and 6.2 (p. 71); the choice is then yours!

As OHTs 6.3–6.5 (72–3) will demonstrate, of the sampling techniques available the questionnaire usually forms the primary data-collecting method. This position is qualified by Cohen and Manion (1989), who state that 'the postal questionnaire is the best form of survey in carrying out an educational enquiry' (109). It is cheap to administer, enables a large group to be targeted and is relatively easy to analyse. Furthermore, we would concur with Walker, who states it 'provides the investigator with an easy (relatively easy) accumulation of data' (1985: 91).

However, users need to be aware of the pitfalls surrounding poorly designed questionnaires. Taking account of the authoritative work by Sudman and Bradburn (1982) and Smith (1975), Narins (1995a, 1995b) has drawn up helpful checklists (OHTs 6.3 and 6.4, p. 72) encompassing question ordering and questionnaire layout.

Having drawn up the outline framework for a questionnaire, it is imperative to ask yourself one final question before launching into the actual audit:

'Will the questionnaire work in the way I have intended?'

Narins (1996), in seeing this important question as the basis of survey pretesting, again offers some pointers (OHT 6.5, p. 73) which provide a helpful aide-memoire. As she concludes, 'the pretest is an element of the survey process that should not be omitted. Without a pretest even experienced researchers can administer a faulty survey, putting into question any results' (8).

Parental perceptions of Moordown school

Representing the first of the external audit undertakings, this survey of parental opinion formed a small-scale research exercise for a higher degree being undertaken at the time (Waller 1993a). It has since featured in an educational journal (Waller 1993b).

This project had several purposes:

- To elicit from parents what they saw as the school's strengths.
- To elicit parental concerns.
- To raise awareness of what this church school has to offer in terms of its perceived, distinctive qualities, and to celebrate these opportunities.

In so doing, it was hoped that parents and the community would be more receptive to the building appeal programme.

Figure 6.1

GUIDE FOR THE CONSTRUCTION OF A QUESTIONNAIRE (After Leedy)

WRITE THE QUESTION CLEARLY AND COMPLETELY IN THE SPACE BELOW	WHAT IS THE BASIC ASSUMPTION UNDERLYING THE QUESTION? HOW DOES THE QUESTION RELATE TO THE RESEARCH PROBLEM?	TYPE OF QUESTION				HOW DO YOU EXPECT TO RELATE THIS QUESTION TO THE RESEARCH EFFORT?
		Multiple Choice	Yes/No Answer	Com-pletion	Counter-check	
Can you identify the 3 main reasons for choosing St John's School?	Gauging the school's strengths.			*		Build upon existing strengths
Can you identify the type of education you would prefer for your child?	Identifying parental priorities regarding preferences in education through applying a ranking system (1-12).	*				Provision of graph illustrating parental priorities; ascertain trends and patterns.
Do you think St John's School markets itself well?	Eliciting parental perspective, remembering that there is always room for improvement.		*			Ascertain whether school's External Relations policy needs review.
What are the school's weaknesses?	Assessing extent of parental concerns before considering appropriate response.			*		Highlighting the school's self-evaluation mode.
What can be done to remedy the situation?	Demonstrating to the parent body that the school values their comments.				*	School seen to be responding to the issues raised.
Do you feel there are too many demands on parents' pockets?	Gauging the level of parental opinion.		*	*		Similar focus for school self-evaluation purposes - a critical issue.
If 'Yes', how can we rectify this whilst avoiding a deficit situation?	Eliciting parental ideas and suggestions and to ascertain whether there are any confusions.				*	Similar focus for school self-evaluation purposes - a critical issue.
What are the things you are happy with about the school?	Encouraging a conscious recognition of the positive facets of the school.			*		Emphasis upon issues raised to be incorporated into a booklet for parents, staff and governors, linking to the preceding fund-raising issue.
... The things that are giving you cause for concern?	When there is a consensus of opinion then remedial action is to be taken.			*		
Would you be happy to recommend St John's School to your friends?	Gauging the general satisfaction of parents with their child's school.		*			Statistically plot the extent of parent satisfaction and whether review necessary.

Figure 6.3

MAIN REASONS FOR CHOOSING ST. JOHN'S OVER OTHER SCHOOLS IN THE AREA

SURVEY UNDERTAKEN WITH THE 1992/93 RECEPTION INTAKE FAMILIES

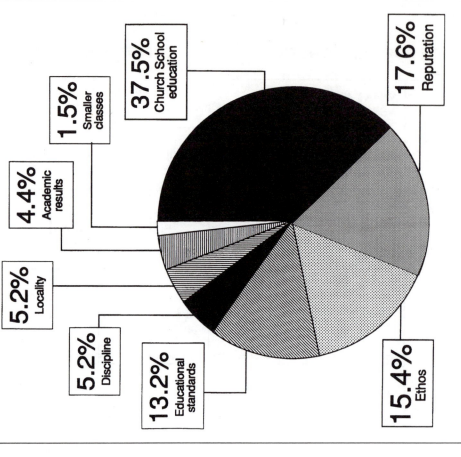

1.5% Smaller classes

4.4% Academic results

37.5% Church School education

5.2% Locality

5.2% Discipline

13.2% Educational standards

17.6% Reputation

15.4% Ethos

SOURCE:
Parental questionnaire survey (February 1993)
Response rate: 88.5%

Figure 6.2

TYPE OF EDUCATION PREFERRED FOR CHILDREN WHEN STARTING SCHOOL

Responses from current and prospective school families:

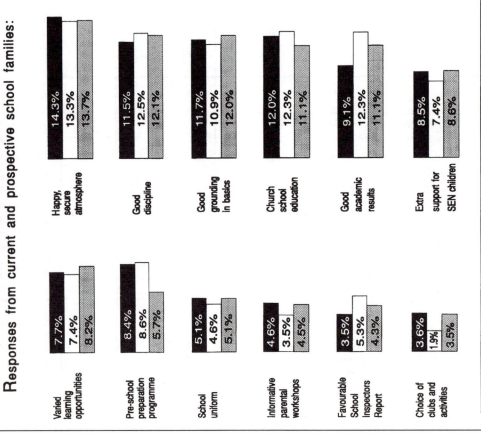

	Prospective families	Reception	NC Yrs 1-6
Happy, secure atmosphere	14.3%	13.3%	13.7%
Good discipline	11.5%	12.5%	12.1%
Good grounding in basics	11.7%	10.9%	12.0%
Church school education	12.0%	12.3%	11.1%
Good academic results	9.1%	12.3%	11.1%
Extra support for SEN children	8.5%	7.4%	8.6%
Varied learning opportunities	7.7%	7.4%	8.2%
Pre-school preparation programme	8.4%	8.6%	5.7%
School uniform	5.1%	4.6%	5.1%
Informative parental workshops	4.6%	3.5%	4.5%
Favourable School Inspectors Report	3.5%	5.3%	4.3%
Choice of clubs and activities	3.6%	1.9%	3.5%

SOURCE:
Parental questionnaire survey (February 1993); overall response rate: 52.7%

58

Using a questionnaire format, suitably colour-coded to distinguish between prospective parents, those with children in the Reception Year and those with older pupils, 351 school families were canvassed. Understandably, the questionnaire targeted at the prospective parents was less wide-ranging. Figure 6.1 (p. 57) shows in detail how the survey questions, pertinent to the audit brief, were analysed. This observed the recommendation from Leedy (1989: 303), who argues that such an approach ensures careful planning of the wording whilst reducing the chance of ambiguity.

At this point it has to be appreciated that in any audit exercise, the role of the head teacher, in partnership with the staff and governors, is crucial in bridging the divide between information and the action resulting from it. Hardie (1991) makes the valid point that they 'must then interpret the information produced ... and make professional decisions which are best for school and client in the short, medium and long term' (56).

The opportunity to rank according to year group did reveal some interesting trends (Fig. 6.2), notably an increased recognition within the Reception age group of the significance of a favourable local education authority (LEA) inspection report that coincided with this survey undertaking. In addition, there is a marked overall consistency in ranking when assessing each of the parental preferences for selecting the school. A *happy, secure atmosphere* was the criterion which parents ranked highest when selecting Moordown. Furthermore, the higher rating given to the school's preschool preparation programme (already outlined in Chapter 3), in the year or two preceding the audit, coincided with significant changes in practice.

The audit findings also appeared to show that parents rated a happy, secure, disciplined environment and caring teachers more highly than impressive academic standards. At the time (1993) it was also interesting to witness, in terms of school effectiveness, a clear correlation between the strengths offered by Moordown (Fig. 6.2) and research undertaken by Mortimer (*Education* 1992), who concluded that:

> most Church of England primary schools performed well academically ... maintained high standards of discipline and behaviour ... were perceptively caring institutions ... successful in encouraging pupils to adopt Christian values ... have a stronger sense of mission ... were intellectually ambitious for their pupils and ... keenly aware of the dignity of individual pupils and teachers. (433)

It is therefore not surprising to find *church school education* ranking as highest (Fig. 6.3, p. 58) in terms of reasons for school choice.

The questionnaire survey also elicited parental concerns and treated them seriously. Those of any significance focused on six issues (Fig. 6.4, p. 60). It is proposed to explore two of these now in more detail – class sizes and playground practice – to demonstrate the ways in which the concerns have been addressed in the intervening years. The issue of 'buildings' has largely been addressed by a massive £1.4m programme of building extension and remodelling (1994–5). Furthermore, in the following chapter we shall be demonstrating the ways in which we have reviewed our 'parental communication' strategies and the sharing of information regarding 'learning programmes'.

Ninety-five per cent of the questionnaire returns challenged the sizes of the classes (at that time up to 33 pupils). In the solutions suggested, the notions of 'smaller classes' and 'more teachers' implied a lack of understanding of the complexities surrounding the funding of the school. Since then, an interactive game for parents (as well as governors and staff) has been devised for use at annual parent meetings. Entitled *Managing the Budget* (1995), it is marketed by Dorset Governor Services. Reproduced here (Fig. 6.5, p. 61) is a copy of an article written by Cleverly and Waller (1994), printed by kind permission of the Director of Education, Libraries and Arts for Dorset. It outlines both the rationale for the game and how it is played. Contact details for obtaining a copy of the pack are also given.

Among the playground concerns (Fig. 6.4), 15 parents raised bullying as a problem. This, as an aspect of pupils' behaviour, has received much attention. However, as the Report from the Office of Her Majesty's Chief Inspector of Schools (1993) suggests, '[bullying] affects even the happiest and most secure of schools' (16). Being difficult to detect and taking place at times

Figure 6.4

ISSUES OF CONCERN / SCHOOL WEAKNESSES
ARISING FROM THE AUDIT SURVEY
Based upon an analysis of questionnaire returns (159 families)
where more than one issue was frequently raised

- **CLASS SIZES -** classrooms too small

  35.8%

- **PLAYGROUND CONCERNS**

  INCIDENTS OF BULLYING

  9.4%

  OVERCROWDED PLAYGROUND - specific reference to infant play area

  6.2%

  LACK OF SUPERVISION

  7.5%

  PLAY EQUIPMENT - its absence; uninteresting playgrounds

  8.2%

- **FUNDRAISING**

  TOO MANY DEMANDS UPON PARENTS

  21.4%

  RECOGNITION THAT REQUESTS ARE INEVITABLE

  9.4%

  DEMANDS NOT CONSIDERED TO BE EXCESSIVE

  13.2%

- **BUILDINGS** - absence of facilities; substandard for today's curriculum

  18.2%

- **LEARNING PROGRAMMES** - certain subject areas (reading, maths); homework; pupil groupings

  11.9%

- **PARENTAL COMMUNICATION / INFORMATION** - teaching programmes, teacher consultations, reporting to parents

  11.3%

POSTSCRIPT

- **NO WEAKNESSES / CONCERNS EXPRESSED**

  26.4%

SOURCE: Parental questionnaire survey (February 1993); overall response rate: 52.7%

Figure 6.5

"EVERYBODY'S NIGHTMARE: THE ANNUAL PARENTS' MEETING"

by Steve Cleverly - Education Officer (LMS) Dorset Education Authority and
Hugh Waller - Headteacher, Moordown St John's CE VA Primary School, Bournemouth

Introduction

As a co-writer of this article, Hugh Waller, as a primary school headteacher, is under no illusion, following the presentation of governor courses on this topic earlier in 1994 (P.S. ... and being repeated in the Spring Term this coming year), that many Governing Bodies are concerned about the apathy apparent among a large number of parents towards this annual statutory meeting.

Both of us are of the opinion, one which is similarly shared by personnel within Dorset Governor Services Unit, that it is important to be proactive with regard to the organisation of the Annual Parents' Meeting (APM). If you, as a governor, concur with this view then the following strategy may be regarded as a 'rescue package' for your next APM.

A possible way forward

Faced with the same dilemma as probably most schools, and yet encouraged by the Governors of Moordown St John's, who had asked us to make the realities of 'managing a school budget more understandable to the lay person, and probably to a number of governors and staff themselves, we set about creating a workshop programme. We started from the premise that we wanted the session to be:
1. interactive;
2. open-ended;
3. one which would take people through the thought processes; and
4. link in the notion of general policy and budgetary decisions being interdependent.

Consideration was given to the fact that, for many people, the concept of a delegated budget is totally alien, and that our package strove, from the outset, to be completely user-friendly.

The Game

It was decided at an early point that we needed to arrange the audience into groups of up to eight people, with governor and staff representation being distributed evenly amongst these groups. As it was, we had around 90 people present around tables, who were positioned prior to the commencement of the APM.

As we were looking for corporate decision-making, the format of the game is based around twenty four printed cards covering every aspect of the school budget with notional costs, as they applied to the size of the school in question, being given. A 'budget card' indicating the total allocation provides the necessary starting information.

The following are illustrated examples of the cards to convey our thinking:
'OPTIMUM CLASS SIZE'
'COVERING FOR ABSENT TEACHING STAFF'
'NUMBER OF EXPERIENCED TEACHERS (INCLUDING DEPUTY AND HEAD)'
'KEEPING THE SCHOOL CLEAN'

Optimum Class Size — Number 33 — Average income per pupil for the year £1,150

Covering for absent teaching staff — Average daily cost £90

Number of experienced teachers (including Deputy and Head) — Average full-time teacher costs £22,000

'BUDGET' CARD — This is your budget total to run this school in the year ahead £

Contract services, (TV, waste disposal, window cleaning, fire safety and security) — Last year's costs £800

Apart from the cards, each group also had an outline budget spreadsheet, along with pencils and calculators, to enable them to easily tabulate their costings. We deliberately used rounded figures ... to make it simple!

In planning this workshop we also devised some 'chance cards', which were made available to those groups who were able to reach a stage of formulating a budget reasonably quickly. If they thought they had finished, they were soon to appreciate the real world, as they wrestled with these unforeseen expenditure outlays.

Each group received their pack following a brief introduction given by Steve Cleverly. He sought to stress:
1. the changes with the introduction of Local Management of Schools;
2. the move away from everything being provided by the LEA and the notion of 30 children equalling one teacher (everyone knows we are now into a more flexible scenario, with governors and head teacher being able to deploy resources as they see fit, yet within the confines of the budget!);
3. the decision-making process, with each school identifying its priorities and associated funding implications;

(some, in fact, did not proceed much further than debating the optimum class size, whilst others moved quickly to reach an agreed budget but, as they were to find out, even credit balances or deficits have to be effectively managed!).

'CHANCE' CARD — There has been an exceptionally cold winter - heating and lighting bills have increased by 50%.

'CHANCE' CARD — This latest pay award for teachers has been announced - each teacher will have a 3% salary increase from September.

'CHANCE' CARD — From this September there will be a reduction in pupil numbers attending this school. Instead of being 464, it will reduce to

Lessons learned

The fact that the session at Moordown St John's generated around 100 minutes of active discussion, which even continued as the audience was ushered out of the doors at 10 pm, is testimony to the level of motivation and interest school budget planning can generate.

To bring the session to a conclusion, each group was invited to table one question for consideration at the plenary session. The questions raised clearly focused upon the heart of school management issues, going well beyond the financial considerations.

The other positive spin-off was that there was an increased understanding of the measureable tensions that governors and headteacher face continually, and the expression of support from the audience has been greatly appreciated at this school, at least. In fact, this was articulated by one of the parents, who commented afterwards in the following vein: " ... Congratulations ... for compiling the budget game for the school's Annual Parents' Meeting. It certainly helped to illustrate many of the issues in the current debate on education. I was so impressed that I went away to give some further thought ... "

As a postscript, negotiations are in hand for this 'budget game' package to be made available through Dorset Governor Services in due course - watch this space for details!

Article reproduced by kind permission of the Director of Education, Libraries and Arts for Dorset

The 'Managing the Budget' game is now available at cost from Dorset Governor Services, Dorset County Council Education, Libraries and Arts Directorate, County Hall, Colliton Park, Dorchester, Dorset, DT1 1XJ.

BUDGET - MOORDOWN ST JOHN'S

within a school day where there is less overt adult supervision, it represents a continuing agenda issue within every school staffroom. As children have a right to feel safe and protected, in our case this school has since re-examined its discipline policy. Linked with this, the pupils and staff have worked collaboratively to produce 'Our School Code' to which everyone subscribes. Both initiatives have significantly reduced these unpleasant incidents. Whilst this, along with the discipline policy, is explored in more detail in the next chapter, given the size of the school community (i.e. 500 pupils) this whole issue remains under constant review.

It is interesting to see how the audit exercise rightly raised the issue about the 'quality' of the supervision offered. This has since been reviewed. Regular in-service training is now offered for our lunchtime supervisory staff to underpin a policy for midday supervision which has also been revised. Implementation and communication of this policy is addressed in the next chapter (Chapter 7, p. 80). The issue of uninspiring playground areas has been explored in two ways. Firstly, a parent has compiled a book of traditional playground games which is available for reference. Secondly, a long-term management strategy to redevelop the play areas is already underway, helped in part by a grant obtained from the British Telecom/Learning through Landscapes School Grounds Award Scheme in 1994.

The resulting strengths, issues and tensions emerging from any audit are worth distilling into a 'SWOT' (Strengths, Weaknesses, Opportunities and Threats) analysis. In the example cited (Fig. 6.6) it reaffirmed the 'agenda for action' and, as Meyerstein (1992) states, 'defin[ed] exactly where the school stands now' (39).

During the intervening years the building programme has been completed and the sum of money required from the school community largely raised. The pursuit of an imaginative fund-raising campaign involving the entire school community that accompanied a promotional brochure is echoed by Metherell (1991): 'the greatest opportunities for increasing income ... arise from making best use of your main assets – people (their expertise) ... pupils ... facilities (buildings and equipment)' (21). Endorsement of Moordown's subsequent actions arising from the 1993 audit is given by Mountfield (1991), who encourages schools to 'seek to promote yourselves and the education you offer ... make yourselves as educationally distinctive as you can – but draw up your own guidelines first' (27).

Informing the school governors

There will be very few schools who do not have to face continual low attendance at the Annual Parents' Meetings. Whilst that has not been an issue for this school, nevertheless the Governing Body, during 1995/96, decided that it was necessary both to ascertain the effectiveness of their existing communication systems among the parent body and to gauge their reactions to the latest Annual Governors' Report. Therefore, adopting the audit principle, we included a single-sided, brief questionnaire with the parental document (Fig. 6.7, p. 64).

When analysing the responses on the aspect of 'communication' (Fig. 6.8, p. 65), whilst it was greatly reassuring to receive overwhelming endorsement for the new-style Report, this was tempered by a majority opinion questioning the governing body's ability to communicate effectively. Judging from the universal support for a brief, termly governors' newsletter and the suggestions to remedy the liaison between governors and parents, the Governing Body has received a clear 'action planning' mandate. From the staff's perspective it was helpful to learn of parental endorsement for better ways of informing about individual subject teaching and the study programmes within each year. How this school is tackling these issues are addressed in the following chapter.

The other facet covered by the questionnaire was eliciting parental feedback regarding the latest Annual Governors' Report. Already a working group of governors is considering how the suggestions can be more effectively addressed in the next issue.

Figure 6.6

SWOT ANALYSIS FOR MOORDOWN ST JOHN'S SCHOOL

STRENGTHS

- Church School
- Happy, secure atmosphere
- Quality of education
- Traditional values
- Varied learning programme
- Effective home-school links
- Increasing oversubscription from prospective families
- Favourable LEA Inspection Report
- Strong discipline
- Support for children with learning needs
- School uniform
- Indoor heated swimming pool
- Playing field with environmental area
- Good relationships with the media
- Effective links with industry/community
- Successful marketing strategies

WEAKNESSES

- Buildings
- No medical room
- Underutilisation of play area
- Lack of support from some families
- Library resource area used as a classroom
- Incidents of bullying in playground
- LMS 'loser' - inheritance of a deficit, which is continuing
- Inconsistencies in playground supervision

THREATS

- Current economic climate
- Current lack of financial support for the school rebuilding scheme
- Possible further delays at DFE level leading to a deferment of the rebuilding programme
- Marketing/competitive action by other schools in the locality

OPPORTUNITIES

- The fact that we are a church school
- Increasing pupil numbers offers financial flexibility in the longer term
- Significant remodelling of the school with the addition of new features (e.g. studio/community room, inner courtyard play area)
- Increased community use of the school's facilities
- Whole school approach to the development of the school site as a learning/recreational resource

Figure 6.7

'WHAT DO YOU THINK OF IT SO FAR?'

* We hope you have enjoyed sharing this year's Annual Report.
* If not, why not? We need to know.
* Maybe it is too long ... too brief ... or did not cover the items that would be of interest to you.
* Please help us to improve future reports by giving us some feedback.
* We have produced the following simple questionnaire to receive your responses.
* All you do is to circle one of the numbers in each line which best reflects your view.
* A few of the questions, however, do require a written response.

	YES	Cannot comment	NO
Communication			
1. If you can remember the previous report(s) can you say if you prefer the latest Report?	1	2	3
2. Do you think the governors of this school communicate important issues adequately?	1	2	3
3. Would you like to receive a brief, termly newsletter from the Governing Body?	1	2	3
4. Are there other ways and times when you would like to meet with one or some of the governors?	1	2	3
5. Would you like more details about how subjects are taught? If so, then this information would be issued as separate leaflets.			
6. Would you also like an outline about what is to be taught in each year group? Again this would appear as a separate information sheet.	1	2	3

This year's Report

1. Which article in the latest Report was of most interest to you?

2. Which article in this latest Report was of least interest to you?

3. Would you like to have specific subjects highlighted in the Report? *(Last year we highlighted ...., this time it is ....)*	1	2	3

4. Is there a particular subject you would like to know more about?
   (Name the subject, if any.)

5. This year's Report has focused upon the decision to raise class sizes given the budgetary constraints. Taking into account the points made, do you think this was the right decision?	1	2	3

6. If you want to make any written comment, please do so.
   (You can also use the other side of the sheet.)

* Many thanks for taking the time to complete this questionnaire, which should be returned to the School Office as soon as possible, and by Friday, ... at the very latest.

* Please indicate the year(s) your child(ren) is (are) in: YEAR(S) ....

Figure 6.8

Survey of Parental Opinion: Communication Systems

Survey completed in September 1996. 74% of the parents responded.

ANNUAL GOVERNORS' REPORT
- preference for latest issue over previous years' report

83%

17%

0%

COMMUNICATION WITH PARENTS
- extent to which this is done adequately at present

34%

8%

58%

TERMLY GOVERNORS' NEWSLETTER
- level of parental interest in new initiative

100%

0%

0%

SUBJECT INFORMATION
- extent of parental support for information in the new way

83%

0%

17%

YEAR GROUP CURRICULUM OUTLINED
- level of support for this new initiative

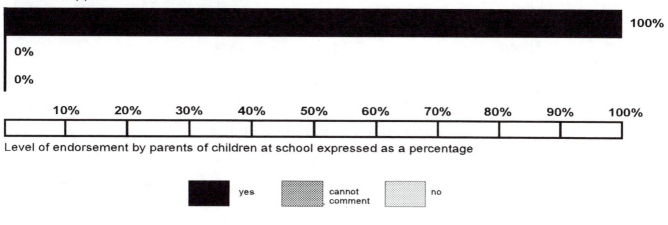

100%

0%

0%

| 10% | 20% | 30% | 40% | 50% | 60% | 70% | 80% | 90% | 100% |

Level of endorsement by parents of children at school expressed as a percentage

yes   cannot comment   no

Figure 6.9 (1)

Moordown St John's School
Effectiveness of Closed Circuit TV Provision

Introduction

You may recall that the School was successful in its bid to the Home Office for installation of CCTV. As part of the conditions pertaining to that successful bid, the School is asked to assess the effectiveness of the system. Consequently, the School, in cooperation with Bournemouth University, is asking you to complete this questionnaire, which has been designed with the help of teachers and parents.

The questionnaire will take approximately three minutes to complete. Please return it to the School Office by **21 April 1997**. Thank you, in advance, for your cooperation.

Next to each answer is a number. When you decide on your answer write the number that belongs to it in the box provided at the side. Just one answer per box please. The computer cannot cope with anything else!

For example   **Bournemouth University is:**

A school	1
A higher education institution	2
A further education institution	3	2

Question 1. In what capacity are you replying to this questionnaire?

Parent	1
Teacher	2
Other staff member	3
Governor	4
More than one of the above	5

☐ 1

Question 2. How many children do you have at the school?

One	1
Two	2
Three	3
Four	4
None	5

☐ 2

if 'none', please go to question 4

Figure 6.9 (2)

Question 3. Which Classes?

Year R   1
Year 1   2
Year 2   3
Year 3   4
Year 4   5
Year 5   6
Year 6   7

First Child ☐ 3
Second Child ☐ 4
Third Child ☐ 5
Fourth Child ☐ 6

Question 4. Security Issues. Please denote the extent of your agreement or disagreement with the following statements:

Agree Strongly   1
Agree   2
Neither Agree nor Disagree   3
Disagree   4
Disagree Strongly   5

On the whole, fears about school security in the UK have been overdone ☐ 7
The main purpose of CCTV is to provide reassurance to parents ☐ 8
The cost of running CCTV would be better spent on other shool resources ☐ 9
don't see how we can run CCTV effectively on a day-to-day basis ☐ 10
Now that we have CCTV, I feel better about leaving the kids at school ☐ 11
CCTV probably works best as a deterrent ☐ 12
School security is not really an issue in Bournemouth ☐ 13
CCTV is the best alternative to turning the school into a 'fortress' ☐ 14
After a while, we shall all quietly forget about CCTV ☐ 15
CCTV is rather like having 'Big Brother' watching you ☐ 16
CCTV should not be use to 'check up' on children in shool for
disciplinary purposes ☐ 17
Realistically, little can be done about school security ☐ 18

Thank you for your co-operation. If you have any additional comments or contributions, please set them out here:

Figure 6.10 (1)

Please can you help? We wish to know more about what you think about our school.

1. Introduction

Our aim is to provide the best all-round learning opportunities for the children within a Christian worshipping setting.

However, we can only do this if we know how you feel about this school.

This questionnaire, which is anonymous, mostly asks you to put ticks or numbers in those boxes which equate with your answer(s). A few questions do require a written response which will also be helpful to us.

It should only take around five minutes to complete.

2. To start with ... some personal information

Indicate the year(s) in which your child(ren) are at this school:

Tick one or more boxes

YrR ☐ Yr1 ☐ Yr2 ☐ Yr3 ☐ Yr4 ☐ Yr5 ☐ Yr6 ☐

How long has your family been associated with this school?

Tick one box

Under 1 yr ☐ 1-3yrs ☐ 4-7 yrs ☐ 8-11 yrs ☐ 12yrs + ☐

3. Our preschool preparation programme

Our preschool preparation programme comprises the following elements listed below. We would like you to rate the usefulness of each element; leave a line blank if you cannot comment:

Circle one number in each line that best reflects your opinion

	VERY GOOD		ACCEPTABLE		NOT HELPFUL
Introductory parents' evening with 'circus' of activities	1	2	3	4	5
Family interview with the headteacher	1	2	3	4	5
Prechool club ... with its 'select and collect' activities	1	2	3	4	5
Starting school profile: 'Early Milestones'	1	2	3	4	5
Reception teacher's home visit	1	2	3	4	5
Can you suggest any further ways we can improve upon our programme?	------------------------------- ------------------------------- -------------------------------				

4. Communication

(a) School Newsletters

	VERY GOOD		ACCEPTABLE		NOT HELPFUL
	Circle the number that best reflects your opinion				
How informative do you find the present newsletters.	1	2	3	4	5

What improvement(s), if any, would you wish to see introduced?

At present newsletters appear usually every fortnight. Would you wish to see this changed? **Tick one box** Yes ☐ No ☐

Only tick one of these boxes if you have said 'Yes' above. **Tick one box if necessary** Weekly ☐ Monthly ☐ Half-termly ☐

(b) Parental information leaflets

Following the parental survey in 1996 this school has responded by producing brief information leaflets on an assortment of topics. How do you rate these?

	VERY GOOD		ACCEPTABLE		NOT HELPFUL
	Circle the number that best reflects your opinion				
	1	2	3	4	5

Our present 'School Prospectus' is shortly to be redesigned. Would you like to see the pages in this publication appearing in the same style as our parent information leaflets? **Tick one box** Yes ☐ No ☐

(c) 1996 Key Stage 2 Performance Tables

In spring of this year information was published, school by school, which showed how Year 6 children performed last summer.

Having sent out guidance information in March, we would like to know how helpful this was to you. *(Spare copies can still be obtained from Reception.)*

	VERY GOOD		ACCEPTABLE		NOT HELPFUL
	Circle one number that best reflects your opinion				
	1	2	3	4	5

(d) Annual School Reports

Each July we issue written school reports describing your child's performance. How do you rate these?

	VERY GOOD		ACCEPTABLE		NOT HELPFUL
	Circle one number that best reflects your opinion				
Accurate picture of my/our child's progress	1	2	3	4	5
Readable style	1	2	3	4	5
Helpful suggestions on ways to assist your child	1	2	3	4	5

Figure 6.10 (2)

5. Let's have your views, please ...

Tell us what you think about these school issues. Give them a rating. If there is a problem, then say in what ways using the space provided.

	VERY GOOD	ACCEPTABLE		NOT HELPFUL
Circle one number that best reflects your opinion				
Class sizes _ _ _ _ _ _ _ _	1	2	3	4	5
Discipline/behaviour _ _ _ _ _ _	1	2	3	4	5
Playground activities _ _ _ _ _	1	2	3	4	5
Lunchtime supervisors _ _ _ _ _	1	2	3	4	5
Fund-raising _ _ _ _ _ _ _ _	1	2	3	4	5
School buildings _ _ _ _ _	1	2	3	4	5
Learning programmes _ _ _ _ _	1	2	3	4	5
Homework _ _ _ _ _ _ _ _ _	1	2	3	4	5

Links with home _

Are there any _
concerns which have _ _ _ _ _ _ _ _ _ _ _ _ _ _ _
not been highlighted? _ _ _ _ _ _ _ _ _ _ _ _ _ _

What can be done _ _ _ _ _ _ _ _ _ _ _ _ _ _ _ _ _
to remedy them? _ _ _ _ _ _ _ _ _ _ _ _ _ _ _ _ _

Why did you choose to send your child to this school? Choose three main reasons from the following list, using '1' for your highest priority

Use '1', '2', and '3' only

☐ Family connections ☐ Child focus
☐ On one site ☐ Church School education
☐ Parental involvement ☐ Discipline
☐ Proximity to school ☐ Educational standards
☐ Reputation ☐ Ethos
☐ Academic results ☐ Facilities

Other reason – please state _
_ _

Now select your criteria for 'a good school'. Please place in order of priority, starting from '1' (the highest) and omitting any you consider unimportant:

Use numbers from '1' onwards:

☐ Choice of clubs and activities
☐ Church School education
☐ Extra support for children with learning needs
☐ Favourable School Inspection Report (1990)
☐ Good academic results
☐ Good discipline
☐ Good grounding in the basics
☐ Happy, secure atmosphere
☐ Informative parental workshops
☐ Preschool preparation programme
☐ School uniform
☐ Varied learning opportunities

6. Dealing with complaints

	(please tick) Have not complained	VERY GOOD	ACCEPTABLE		NOT HELPFUL
		Circle one number that best reflects your opinion			
How good are we at handling complaints?	☐	1	2	3	4	5
		VERY	ACCEPTABLE		NOT
Do we respond promptly if this has ever arisen for you?	☐	1	2	3	4	5

7. Community

	EXCELLENT	GOOD		IN NEED OF IMPROVEMENT
	Circle one number that best reflects your opinion			
How would you rate this school's reputation within the community?	1	2	3	4	5

Say what you would like
to see this school doing _ _ _ _ _ _ _ _ _ _ _ _ _ _ _ _
to enhance its reputation: _ _ _ _ _ _ _ _ _ _ _ _ _ _ _
_ _

8. Finally ...

Would you be happy to recommend our school to your friends?

Tick one box

Yes ☐   Yes, with reservations ☐   No ☐

Thank you for taking the time to complete this questionnaire. We will let you know the results after we have processed the information. This will be at the Annual Parents' Meeting in September 1997.

Monitoring the school's security initiatives

Security is now very much a priority issue for all schools in the aftermath of the nationally reported tragedies. Surveying parental opinion provides a means of reviewing its existing procedures, prioritising new initiatives and assessing the impact of new schemes.

For Moordown, success in the Home Office's CCTV (Closed Circuit Television) Challenge Competition 1996, coupled with partial funding from Dorset County Council's Risk Management Support Group, has led to the installation of a security camera system at nominal cost. In order to gauge the value of this additional tier in the school's security management strategy, an external evaluation was commissioned. An initial focus group session, involving representatives drawn from the school community, then informed the subsequent questionnaire (Fig. 6.9, p. 66–7), reproduced by kind permission of Bournemouth University.

Revisiting the external relations audit

Four years on from the initial parental survey the staff and governors consider it appropriate for the exercise to be repeated. As the latest questionnaire (Fig. 6.10, p. 68–9) demonstrates, similar questions feature again. However, the school's recent re-focus on 'communication' has prompted some additional questions, including the opportunity to elicit feedback following the publication of the 1996 Key Stage 2 Performance Tables. This latest audit survey, completed in the summer term 1997, was reported at the Annual Parents' Meeting in the autumn. Graphical representation of the comparative data again featured prominently for the purposes of impact and conveying the latest position.

Summary

There is no doubt that parents can provide a valuable source of reaction to school practices and procedures, which should never be ignored.

Remember ... all customer surveys are about the same thing:

1. *What do you think about us?*
2. *How could we do better?*

Having amassed the responses from the audit undertaking, the school is then empowered to act upon the evidence emerging, sharing this with staffing colleagues and with governors. However, it is equally imperative that the survey audience receives regular feedback on the action being taken as a consequence.

QUANTITATIVE SURVEYS

TYPE	ADVANTAGES	DISADVANTAGES
Questionnaire (all types)	* Can give a clear consensus message * Uses graphics for impact	* Requires a great deal of thought and planning * Can get bogged down in statistics * Usually sets the agendas for more questions
Questionnaire (distributed for completion later)	* Easy and quick to administer * Everyone answers the same questions * Responses easy to collate * Option for responses to be made anonymously * Can encompass a wide range of school issues	* Those completing the questionnaires can interpret questions differently * Open to completion without much reflection * If a low response rate, feedback may be unrepresentative * Does not allow for further questioning and probing
Questionnaire (completed when handed out)	* Displays all of the above advantages * Response rate is high * Queries regarding questions can be addressed at the time	* Does not allow much time for reflection

Adapted from the schedule appearing in the *School Audit Manual* (1997) by Crix & Ladbrooke (p.3). Reproduced with the permission of the authors and the publisher, Pitman Publishing.

QUALITATIVE SURVEYS

TYPE	ADVANTAGES	DISADVANTAGES
Individual Interviews	* Usually provides the clearest messages * Provides opportunity to probe issues in depth * Interviewee can feel that his or her views are valued	* Extremely time-consuming both in managing the interview sessions and in transcribing the recorded tapes * Difficult to manage results * Interviewees may tell you what you want to hear * Too easy to pick and choose ancedotes to suit your purpose
Group Meetings	* Less time-consuming than individual interviews, although still have to be recorded * Provides an accurate record of key issues raised by interested parties * Simple to analyse and pinpoint recurring issues * Real insights can be achieved through use of techniques such as brainstorming * A variety of views can be explored and any uncertainties addressed	* Open to the possibility of being dominated by one or two individuals * Group's over-enthusiasm could lead to hasty decisions being taken * Without a wide-ranging checklist, may not cover all that needs to be considered

Adapted from the schedule appearing in the *School Audit Manual* (1997) by Crix & Ladbrooke (pp.3-4). Reproduced with the permission of the authors and the publisher, Pitman Publishing.

QUESTIONNAIRE SURVEY
Layout tips

* Create layout which is neat, professional, carefully designed and uncluttered

* Have eye-catching, attractive cover so that respondents notice the survey

* Carefully choose typeface to:
  - maximise legibility
  - differentiate between instructions and questions

* Start with brief introduction describing:
  - survey's purpose
  - topics to be covered
  - how results to be used

* Make instructions easy to understand ... and user-friendly

* Provide plenty of space for questions and answers - makes reading easier

* Make survey easy to complete by ensuring:
  - numbers to be circled sufficiently far apart
  - consistent positioning of response boxes

* See that questions are numbered clearly

* Give careful consideration to ordering, numbering and grouping of questions

* Arrange questionnaire in booklet form where there are multiple pages

* Leave plenty of room for respondents to write answers to open-ended questions; do not supply lines as this forms a constraint

* With interviewer-administered surveys, print interviewer instructions in different font or in italics

* Remember to conclude questionnaire with 'Thank You' statement

* Ideas adapted from research publications by Cohen & Manion (1989, 3rd. ed.), Narins (1995a, 1995b), Smith (1975), Sudman & Bradburn (1982) and Youngman (1978)

QUESTIONNAIRE SURVEY
Ordering tips

* Keep initial questions simple, of high interest value; treat as warming-up exercise

* Enlist respondent's interest in survey from very beginning

* Start with general questions ... moving on to more specific ones gradually

* Do not begin either with an open-ended question or one which respondents might feel has 'right' answer

* Group questions into sections

* Position sections in logical order

* Introduce each new section with sentence or phrase

* Place riskier questions later in survey; if respondent refuses to continue then less information lost

* Position demographic questions at end of questionnaire; this keeps respondent's mind on purpose of survey from outset

* Minimise number of times when response triggers the missing questions

* Offer mix of multiple choice and open-ended questions where appropriate

* Remember ... open-ended questions allow respondents to air their opinion, rather than simply describe their behaviour

* Avoid listing different attributes in ways which encourage respondent to select initial few as being 'correct choice'; either randomly or alphabetically order them, stating this in the instructions

* If questionnaire targeted at different survey audiences, print several versions if possible.

* Ideas adapted from research publications by Narins (1995), Smith (1975) and Sudman & Bradburn (1982)

QUESTIONNAIRE SURVEY
Pretesting tips

Planning
* Ensure pilot group representative of eventual target population

* Advantage in using same people for pretest and actual survey - 'ownership' factor in something they have helped to construct

* Number of pretests determined by assortment of factors; with new survey, conduct minimum of two, one if questions administered before

* Conduct all pretests under same conditions as final questionnaire

* Assess responses to open-ended questions - if few given then check wording, positioning and spacing for replies

* Profusion of 'Don't Know' responses imply poorly constructed question, unclear or inappropriate wording

* Little or no variation in responses may imply question not as clear as intended

* Check observance of instructions, such as 'missing' sections where appropriate

* If no weaknesses uncovered, still presume a problem ... rather than perfection!

Interviewer
* Encourage openness from pilot group to questionnaire design and format

* Be on look-out for possible confusion, ambiguity or hesitation by respondents

* Gather as much insight from participants as possible about:
  - flow of questions
  - ability to complete questionnaire
  - whether their attention held
  - individual interpretation of specific questions

* Keep 'balance' in mind when suggestions proffered - you the ultimate authority!

Procedure
* Make respondents aware they are participating in a pretest

* Time completion of survey by respondents - it should not take too long!

7 Sharing curricular and organisational practice

An overview

Effective communication by a school, whether oral or written, is considered essential if parents are to be realistically involved. However, as a national survey of local education authorities and interviews with a sample of parents (Jowett and Baginsky 1991) has ascertained, there is still considerable room for improvement. The researchers state that:

> while there were meetings held for parents to explain the curriculum, or how something was being taught, these were frequently inadequately planned and failed to convey information in a clear and accessible form ... More attention needs to be given to the presentation of written communication. Many of the school handouts and other documentation for parents ... were not particularly informative and were written in a style that could itself discourage parents. (202)

This chapter offers a means whereby a school can project its image, through the visual and written form, to complement its ethos and vision. Time well spent in this area will, as the authors have found, pay untold dividends.

Space only permits examples to feature in this book – the full range may be obtained from Primary Headstart Publications (see Notes section at the front of this book). By making information available for copying and adaptation within the purchasing institution, we hope we have adhered to the maxim of 'providing quality and clarity of information for the school's parents'.

Those first impressions ...

A school's performance in the league tables, the style and content of its prospectus and Annual Governors' Report, along with the outcome of an OFSTED inspection, all influence parental perceptions of a school. Whilst these shape its reputation, a more fundamental issue exists. Of prime importance is the school's image.

In an extremely practical and resourceful publication by Alexander *et al.* (1995) on home–school policies, this very telling remark is made: *first impressions are lasting impressions* (49). Making a good impression on parents, whether prospective or otherwise, represents a long-term investment which can have innumerable benefits for the school community. However, as Hepworth (1996) contends, promoting a positive image is 'about managing that reputation and shaping what people think and say about you' (30).

To create a lasting impression entails a methodical consideration of all the issues. Hepworth (1996: 32) offers a useful checklist to assist in this worthwhile task. Furthermore, it would be sensible for a school's staff to devote staff meeting time, with governor representation too, and/or canvass parental opinion through a questionnaire (refer to Chapter 6 for detailed guidance) in exploring this aspect. The accompanying schedules (OHT 7.1, p. 92–3) provide some useful pointers to aid this internal review. However, Alexander *et al*, (1995: 24–5) provides a sample parental questionnaire. Suitably adapted and with an appropriate acknowledgement to the source, this should generate a wealth of helpful and useful evidence.

Saying what the school is about

Schools will see this as being presented within the legally required school prospectus, which has to be published annually for parents and prospective parents. The timing of its publication is also important in that it must appear at least six weeks before the closing date for admissions for the forthcoming school year. This will clearly vary from school to school but will be at some point during the autumn term.

Furthermore, details of what needs to be included are outlined in regulations linked to a succession of Education Acts (all subsumed into the 1996 Education Act) along with more recent departmental circulars (1994 and 1996). It is suggested that the reader refers to helpful guidance from the Department for Education and Employment (1996), which will allow an audit of the school's existing publication to see how it compares with the requirements governing primary schools, both statutory and non-statutory.

Similarly, the significance for parents of the prospectus when shortlisting prospective schools for their child(ren) emanates from 'The Parent's Charter' (DES 1991). This encourages parents to be active and influential in their child's education. It makes clear that the vehicles for information from schools are the prospectuses which 'have to tell you about the aims of the school and the subjects and other activities offered in each school year ... You can ask for a prospectus free from any school' (6).

However, before considering in greater detail the content and subsequent production issues, it is worth having regard for some guiding principles that this publication embodies, especially for prospective parents. Firstly, as Devlin and Knight (1990) stress, it can be regarded as a mechanism for 'public relations and marketing for schools' (iv). In re-echoing the theme of 'first impressions being all important', Devlin and Knight claim that the school prospectus 'is the most important statement about your school' (62), in that it provides important evidence about school policy and how this is interpreted in practice, as well as affirming the values it seeks to uphold in its pupils. This notion is developed further by Copeland (1994) who sees the prospectus as providing 'access to what schools regard as influential in the portrayal of their policies and also the relative emphasis which their policies are given by themselves' (239). Furthermore, the prospectus provides its readers with a 'window display' of the school. Knight (1992) articulates this view thus: 'prospectuses tell the world how schools want to be seen' (56). However, as will be only too apparent to head teachers, staff and governors studying this publication, there is a greater awareness on the part of prospective parents about schooling opportunities. Whilst we can challenge the previous government's assertion that all parents have 'choice' for their child(ren), nevertheless it is imperative that the prospectus represents an accurate, honest and simple portrayal of the school's philosophy, organisation and practice. The difficulty for parents is in being able to separate out aspirations from the reality simply from this publication. Common sense dictates that seeing the school 'in action' provides valuable complementary evidence.

Whilst the detailed content of the school prospectus is a matter for a school's Governing Body, in consultation with its head teacher and staff, it is also helpful if consideration is given to the aide-memoire printed as OHT 7.2 (p. 94). We hope that those responsible for the authorship and design of this statutory publication will recognise that the school prospectus needs to reflect amply how 'communication' is perceived within your school. For it to be a truly worthwhile publication it must complement the corporate image you are seeking to portray to your parent community.

The design style is also a matter of personal choice. However, within each local education authority people will be available to give advice, as well as handling the design and printing at a negotiated fee. The Professional Development Services business unit within Dorset County Council's Education, Libraries and Arts Directorate is just one example. With their permission, a helpful agreement form (Fig. 7.1, p. 76) is included to assist at this stage in the production process. An external incentive to produce a worthwhile prospectus has, in the past, been provided by the annual *Times Educational Supplement*'s School Prospectus Award Competition.

Further on-entry information

The development of a foundation curriculum, coupled with admission arrangement changes, has also prompted schools to consider providing parents with information specifically targeted at their child's first year of statutory schooling. While some may argue that this can be included in the school prospectus, because of its focused content there is sense in compiling a

Figure 7.1

SCHOOL PROSPECTUS AGREEMENT FORM

* DfEE Checklist   Yes ☐   No ☐

* User Friendly   Yes ☐   No ☐

	Sample A	Sample B	Sample C

* Paper type matt sample x ☐ gloss sample y ☐ weight ☐   Sample A ☐   Sample B ☐   Sample C ☐

* Ground colour paper [＿＿＿]

* Ground colour card [＿＿＿]

* Photocopied   Black only   Yes ☐ No ☐   FULL colour page   Yes ☐ No ☐

   Black only   Yes ☐ No ☐   1 extra colour ☐ [＿＿＿]

   2 extra colours ☐ [＿＿＿]

   FULL colour [＿＿＿]

* Bind type

Slide binder		Stab stitched		Saddle stitched	
Stab stitched & tape		Spiral bound		Ring binder	

* Bind colour

* Number of copies insides

* Number of copies covers

* Format

Landscape

A5	A4	A3

Portrait

A5
A4
A3

* Number of sides SB, ST ST, ST & T, SPB RB   [8] [10] [12] [14] [16] [18] [20]

SS [8] [12] [16] [20] [24] [28]

* TEXT FONT STYLE [＿＿＿]   * TEXT FONT SIZE [＿＿＿]
* TITLE FONT SIZE [＿＿＿]
* BULLETS STYLE [＿＿＿]   * BULLETS SIZE [＿＿＿]

Italic required   Pages ☐ ☐ ☐ ☐

		Yes	No		Yes	No
* Children's drawings original	BW	☐	☐	Colour	☐	☐
reproductions	BW	☐	☐	Colour	☐	☐
* Photos originals	BW	☐	☐	Colour	☐	☐
reproductions	BW	☐	☐	Colour	☐	☐

Signed ....   Date ....

With acknowledgement to the Professional Development Services, Dorset County Council Education Libraries & Arts Directorate

Figure 7.2

RECEPTION YEAR
Information for Parents

* **Introducing .... the staff in your child's first year**
  Teaching staff; Support staff

* **The teaching experiences we offer ....**
  Personal and Social Development; Language and Literacy; Mathematics;
  Knowledge and Understanding of the World; Creative Development;
  Physical Development

* **Recording and Reporting**
  Keeping records; Reporting progress; Reporting to parents

* **Learning Support**
  Our policy; What we offer

* **Admissions**
  Our policy; The admissions procedure; Timing of children's entry into school

* **Home -school links**

* **Discipline - it's all about 'being good'**
  Our policy; What we are looking for

* **Do you need to complain?**
  What to do first ...; Sometimes it's a matter of misunderstanding;
  There's help at hand ...; What if you still disagree with this school?

* **In and around our school**
  Our premises; The equipment we use

* **Keeping everyone safe**
  Our policy; Safe practices

* **Equal Opportunities**
  What it means; We have a policy

* **Financial contributions**
  Our Swimming Pool Fund; The Diocesan Capitation and School Welfare Fund
  Our School Rebuilding Scheme Fund

* **Term and Holiday Dates**

* **External School Inspections**

Figure 7.3

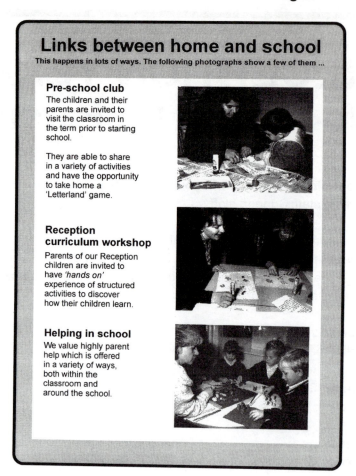

Links between home and school
This happens in lots of ways. The following photographs show a few of them ...

Pre-school club
The children and their parents are invited to visit the classroom in the term prior to starting school.

They are able to share in a variety of activities and have the opportunity to take home a 'Letterland' game.

Reception curriculum workshop

Parents of our Reception children are invited to have *'hands on'* experience of structured activities to discover how their children learn.

Helping in school
We value highly parent help which is offered in a variety of ways, both within the classroom and around the school.

publication specifically for reception parents. The headings and sub-headings are outlined in Figure 7.2 (p. 77). Each forms a differently coloured broadsheet that appears in one of the file pockets. Given this flexibility, individual pages can easily be amended. Figure 7.3 provides an example of suggested design, layout and content.

Articulating curriculum and organisational practice

While the school prospectus represents the primary means whereby curriculum policy and practice is communicated to parents in summative form, Moordown has made use of 'parent partnership' funding (explained in Chapter 2, p. 5) to develop user-friendly, readable leaflets. Each offers more precise and focused information. This initiative arose as a response to parental views expressed in the 1996 survey (reported previously in Chapter 6, p. 65). Examples of the type of publication are the ones on 'Science' (Booklet 7.1, p. 95) and 'Lifting the Lid off Assessment' (Booklet 7.2, p. 96). The complete range can be purchased from Primary Headstart Publications (see Notes section at the front of this book).

Judging from feedback emerging from OFSTED primary inspections, curricular information should also be made available to parents in a year group format. As Laar (1997) reports, 'it is now commonplace for schools to give parents a broad outline of the educational experiences their children will encounter over ... a term' (328). Not only does this serve to inform parents but the knowledge imparted also provides a helpful framework 'to enable and encourage them to support their children's work and contribute in various ways to the planned learning activities' (328). This school takes a similar view, as can be gleaned from the two examples included (Booklet 7.3 – Year 1; Booklet 7.4 – Year 4: p. 97–8). Quite naturally the content is particular to Moordown, yet it offers a helpful framework whereby interested primary, first, junior and middle schools can devise their own.

Homework represents a topic that continues to attract media attention, fuelled by recent political debates. The Report from the Office of Her Majesty's Chief Inspector of Schools

Figure 7.4

'PRIMARY HEADSTART
- KEY STAGE 1
HOME STUDY PACK'

'PRIMARY HEADSTART
- KEY STAGE 1
HOME STUDY PACK'

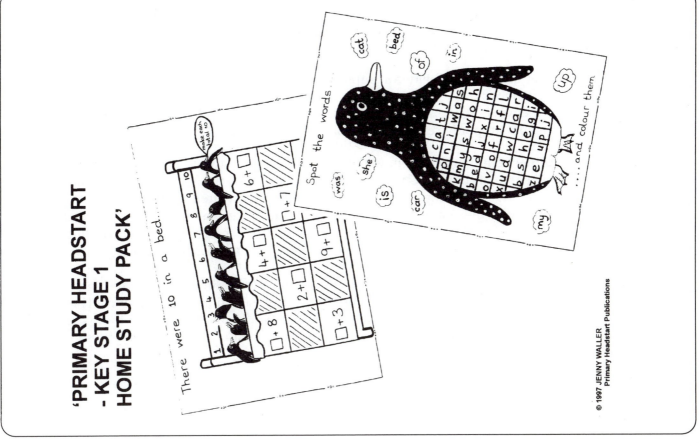

(OFSTED 1995) makes the valid point that one of its purposes is to 'create a firm partnership between parents and teachers in relation to children's learning' (4). The mandate to review Moordown's approach to homework came as a consequence of the 1993 parental survey (reported in Chapter 6, p. 55–73). Since then our school's home study programme now boasts its own 'ACORN' logo with an accompanying parental guide (Booklet 7.5, p. 99) which explains the purposes of homework, the gradual increase in quantity over the seven primary years, when it should be undertaken, where children should study and the parental role in providing assistance and support. Like other school-focused initiatives it is accompanied by an activity workshop programme for parents where we share how children learn and the optimum conditions for learning at home and in school. We have been influenced by Hannon (1992) who presents a cogent argument for getting teachers involved in children's home learning by suggesting there should be 'opportunities for dialogue ... and feedback loops to inform future practice' (6).

At the time of going to press, Moordown is still evaluating the project, taking account of the perceptions of the key players involved – teaching staff, parents, governors and pupils. In the meantime, research evidence commissioned by the Department for Education and Employment (Barber *et al.* 1997), and targeted at the secondary phase, is suggesting that a rigorous approach to homework within a better managed school is coalescing to produce higher performance standards. While the subject remains ripe for continued debate, we believe there is a keen interest among primary schools in using published homework ideas. A home study pack focusing on the three core subjects for Key Stage 1 is available from Primary Headstart Publications. Sample activity sheets appear in Figure 7.4 (p. 79).

While administering medication remains a voluntary role (and *not* a legal duty) for school staff, schools are required to have in place effective management systems to support individual pupils with medical needs. The recent publication of guidance material by the Department of Education and Employment and Department of Health, entitled: *Supporting Pupils with Medical Needs* (1996), provides a 'prompt' to schools in reviewing their practices. Having completed the exercise at Moordown St John's it was felt appropriate to communicate to parents, in clear terms, the way we handle medicines and accidents (Fig. 7.5; the actual leaflets appear in the pack obtainable from Primary Headstart Publications). Strongly influencing this decision is the fact that there are very clearly defined responsibilities for key school personnel, as well as the employer (that is the local education authority or the Governing Body), the medical fraternity and the parents. The DfEE/DoH guidance expresses it in these terms:

> It is important that responsibility for pupils' safety is clearly defined and that each person involved with pupils with medical needs is aware of what is expected of them. Close cooperation between schools, parents, health professionals and other agencies will help provide a suitably supportive environment for pupils with medical needs. (DfEE/DoH 1996: 2)

Providing a further control mechanism in the communication between home and school is the use of a printed parental consent form (Fig. 7.6, p. 82) regarding the administration of medicine and/or treatment. This was only introduced having secured written approval from the local education authority at the outset. For a school staff there are issues of safety management, administration procedures, the drawing up of individual health care plans and dealing with specific medical conditions to address. *Supporting Pupils with Medical Needs* (1996) considers them all.

Other topics, presented in illustrative leaflet form and addressing similar high-profile issues in parents' minds, include 'School Discipline' and 'Lunchtime Supervision'. The latter appears in this book (Booklet 7.6, p. 100), yet all can be obtained as part of the pack from Primary Headstart Publications. It is then possible for a reader to 'customise' these to suit their school's needs.

Figure 7.5

ACCIDENTS AT SCHOOL/MEDICINES AT SCHOOL

Figure 7.6

Moordown St John's Primary School
PARENTAL CONSENT FORM
THE ADMINISTRATION OF MEDICINE/TREATMENT

PLEASE PRINT
Child's name:..

Address:
Child's mother: .... Child's father (if different): ....

Home telephone number:
Child's mother:... Child's father (if different): ....

Parents' work telephone number:
Child's mother: .... Child's father:...

Medical contacts:
GP's name: .... GP's telephone number: ....

Hospital consultant: .... Hospital telephone: ....

The above child has been identified as having: ....
....

Please tick appropriate box:

☐ My child will be responsible for the self-administration of medicines as directed below.

☐ I agree to designated members of staff administering medicines/providing treatment to my
child as directed below or, in the case of an emergency, as staff consider necessary.

Signed: .... (Parent/Guardian)   Date: ....

Name of Medicine	Dose	Frequency/Times

* In the case of asthma or diabetes, separate information cards are to be completed; these are obtained from the School Office.

Special instructions: ....

Allergies: ....

Other prescribed medicines child is taking at home:

....

Date received:	
Copies to: First Aid file Parent/Guardian	*(Date)*

Figure 7.7

FOUNDATION CURRICULUM WORKSHOP
Planning notes for organisers

Estimated timing	Workshop sections	Organisational details
10 minutes	'Ice-breaking' activity	In groups parents reflect upon their responses to three questions: 1. *'What are your recollections of your school when a young child?'* 2. *'What response do you get when asking your child: "What did you do at school today?"'* 3. *'Why do teachers encourage children to "play" in the classroom?'* *(all the above appear as Figs. 7.8-7.10, from which question cards can be made)*

15 minutes	Unpicking the Reception curriculum	1. Leader input outlining key purposes of structured learning
		
		2. Expand on the 'Desirable Learning Outcomes' and how these lead naturally from nursery education to early years' practice; at this point introduce Booklet 7.7
		
		3. Reception staff expand upon the following using visual examples (e.g. slides, video evidence):
		   - *socio-dramatic play*
		   - *small world play*
		   - *block play*

60 minutes	And now... the activity tasks	1. Before parents commence a set of nine tasks (see Fig. 7.11), parents reminded of the time limit for each activity (i.e. 5 minutes, denoted by bell/whistle sounding, followed by 1 minute to complete the recording sheet, Fig. 7.12) 2. When completing each activity task, parents reminded about scoring each one using the information pamphlet as a point of reference (Booklet 7.7)
20 minutes	What have we learned?	1. Opportunity given to the participants, once they have returned to the main meeting point, to offer their point, to offer their reactions to the various tasks completed 2. Reiterate the point that the workshop session, by its very nature, can only offer a brief snapshot of the Reception Year's 'foundation curriculum'

ADDITIONAL ORGANISATIONAL NOTES

* Name labels - to make 'introductions' easier

* Overhead projector (OHP), TV/video recorder and/or slide projector and large screen (according to requirements)

* Seating in main arena in groups (tables optional), each having clear visibility of presenters and TV monitor/screen (if required)

* Preparation of school resources (OHTs, slides, video evidence), question cards (Figs. 7.8-7.10), selected activity tasks (Fig. 7.11), recording sheet (Fig. 7.12) and reference leaflet (Booklet 7.7)

Figure 7.8

What are your recollections of your school when a young child?

Figure 7.9

What response do you get when asking your child: *'What did you do at school today?'*?

Figure 7.10

Why do teachers encourage children to *'play'* in the classroom?

Learning opportunities for parents

Creating still further a climate of learning for parents are the activity workshops, whose programme at Moordown continues to expand and diversify. Whether it has a curriculum subject or a specific year group or organisational focus, the intention is for it to be seen as a valued activity.

One example is the school's 'Foundation Curriculum' workshop which is offered to parents of the initial Reception Year intake within the first month or so of their children starting. How many times do we hear from parents that on asking their children 'What have you done at school today?' the responses are invariably negative (for example: 'I can't remember,' 'I played all day,' or 'Nothing!')? To address these confusing messages, a workshop with a significant bias towards practical activity (Fig. 7.7, p. 83) offers a systematic insight into the role of 'play' within the early years curriculum. This in turn is then cross-referenced to the 'Desirable Learning Outcomes' that feature prominently within the Reception Year which are explained in another parental guide (Booklet 7.7, p. 101).

Parental feedback remains positive, as the following quotation confirms:

> The evening ... provided all our answers. It is delightful to be able to experience what our child is doing at school. We found this so much more informative than a talk would have been. I am so encouraged when I compare this with my own schooling. Your outlook is modern and approachable and, going by our experiences ... I feel sure that our children will learn by enjoyment and interest. The evening also showed us ... how we can best build on the work done by school by reinforcing the same principles at home. I have certainly gained some new ideas! (Letter to the head teacher, dated 27 February 1997)

Another workshop, this time addressing the subject of managing child asthma within the school setting, appears in journal articles written by Waller (1993c, 1996). Essentially the programme revolves around an educational workshop package entitled: 'Asthma: True or False Game' (Waller *et al.* 1992). Its rationale is visually portrayed in Figure 7.13 (p. 88). Presented jointly by a medical practitioner and educationalist, this interactive workshop approach has been shown

Figure 7.11

FOUNDATION CURRICULUM WORKSHOP
Suggested activity tasks

Theme	Activity tasks
1. Socio-dramatic play	* Parent and baby's visit to the clinic
	* Using the characters and play items, create a story about the play park
2. Mathematics	* Using 'Smarties', count/sort them, make pattern picture; investigate tube's properties
	* Using playdough, make a pond and place five tadpoles in it
3. Science	* Investigate properties of dry sand using range of equipment; allow sand to trickle through fingers - hear anything?
	* Taking each object in turn, guess if it will float or sink and then compare with test situation
4. PE/PSE	* Activities (a) using small apparatus and (b) completing simple repeat exercises
5. Music	* Working with claves, woodblocks and xylophone, create 'conker falling' sounds; demonstrate slow/fast fall
	* Working with scrapers, shakers and bangers, create variable sounds which partner copies; reverse roles
6. Geography/History	* Using equipment, create a model farm; draw plan of it
	* Draw plan of a room in their house
	* Self-portraits - as a baby and now
7. Design & Technology	* Using wallpaper design examples, create one's own using equipment provided
	* Looking at card designs, create one's own using equipment/materials supplied
8. Art	* Using brushes/implements/paints (either red/white or yellow/blue), create pattern design
9. IT	* Use of appropriate computer software to practise use of arrow keys/space bar and/or mouse/bin

ADDITIONAL ORGANISATIONAL NOTES

* Focus for each activity task flexible, this being governed by available equipment/space, etc.

* Prepare instruction cards for each activity with required resources/equipment readily available

* Make use of additional support staff to oversee and/or assume teaching role in certain of the activity tasks

Figure 7.12

FOUNDATION CURRICULUM WORKSHOP
Parental recording sheet

Place the number of the activity completed under the appropriate 'areas of learning'

Personal and Social Development

Language and Literacy

Mathematics

Knowledge and Understanding of the World

Physical Development

Creative Development

Figure 7.13

'ASTHMA: TRUE OR FALSE GAME '

Joint Authors:

HUGH WALLER MA (Ed) B Ed(Hons) FRSA
Headteacher
Moordown St. John's CE Primary School,
Bournemouth.

PETER JOHNSTON FRCP
Consultant Paediatrician
West Dorset General Hospitals NHS Trust,
Dorchester, Dorset.

DAVID BELLAMY MBE BSc MRCP MRCCGP
General Practitioner
The James Fisher Medical Centre,
Bournemouth.

Introduction

As headteacher of a primary school with over 500 pupils, of whom over 12% have asthma, Hugh Waller, one of the co-authors and a late onset asthma sufferer himself has, for some time, recognised the management issues involved, in that children with asthma have particular needs which require addressing. Successful medical research points to under-diagnosis and treatment, which has impaired school performance. To address this, a 'School Asthma Policy' was developed in 1991 at Moordown St. John's CE Primary School in Bournemouth by Hugh Waller, with welcome assistance from several general practitioners in the locality.

The Game . . .
and how it has been used

The game pack comprises photocopy master sheets of the cards and base sheet, along with printed instructions. It is available, at cost (£2.00) from the school address above.

The sixteen cards each have a statement and it is up to the user to decide upon a response - 'true' or 'false'.

ASTHMA "TRUE or FALSE" GAME
AN AID TO RAISING AWARENESS ABOUT CHILD ASTHMA THROUGH INFORMED DISCUSSION

HUGH WALLER in association with PETER JOHNSTON and DAVID BELLAMY

Background to the . . . 'Asthma: True or False Game'

As a result of the introduction of a 'School Asthma Policy', it was necessary:-

(a) to develop an effective training package to increase knowledge and understanding of asthma;

(b) to change staff and parent attitudes towards the management of asthma in school;

(c) to develop confidence among <u>all</u> staff in handling children with asthma; and

(d) to encourage confidence among the parents of these children about the school's approach.

The game has been used in meetings with representatives from the education and medical professions as well as school governors and parents.

By distributing the cards and inviting a response to the statements, a dialogue is set up between the presenters and the audience.

Why was this model developed in preference to other in-service approaches?

1. It moves away from pure didactic teaching.
2. It is interactive in its approach.
3. It addresses the needs of the learner.
4. It caters for all levels of school personnel - headteachers, class teachers and support staff.
5. It offers a flexible presentation, which can adapt to the needs of its audience.
6. It employs a variety of presentation methods - short, illustrated talks, practical demonstrations . . . with audience participation throughout.

Conclusion

In the initial piloting of this Game, it is the considered view of its authors that the audiences gain a clearer understanding of what asthma is and how it can be appropriately managed within school.

Now proven by research (Waller, 1995) this interactive workshop approach does contribute to lasting changes in staff attitudes towards asthmatic children. Its effectiveness is in marked contrast to didactic presentation method or the provision of literature.

According to Peter Johnston, one of the co-authors:
' . . . if the game is taken seriously and used well, then it should improve the care of asthma in childhood, both in school and out of it.'

(Waller 1995) to contribute to lasting changes in staff attitudes towards asthmatic children. Employing a variety of presentational approaches, the programme mirrors a strategy articulated earlier (refer to Chapter 5, p. 26–7). As Peter Johnston says, 'if the game is taken seriously and used well, then it should improve the care of asthma in childhood, both in school and out of it' (Waller *et al.* 1992: 2).

Guiding parents to help their children's learning at school

To complement the leaflets on curricular and organisational topics, Moordown's parents have recently requested helpful 'pointers' in the specific areas of literacy and numeracy.

Leaflets have been devised which are supported by activity workshop programmes. Figure 7.14 (p. 90) offers a montage showing 'Reading Together: a helpful guide to fluent reading'. Two leaflets offer other systematic guidance in the area of mathematics. Each provides tried and tested examples that parents can manage with confidence. These titles feature in the pack obtainable, at cost, from Primary Headstart Publications.

Moving on to senior school

Within local education authorities in England and Wales children transfer from one phase of education to another at different ages. However, there remain underlying issues that are pertinent whenever children face a change of school. A consensus exists within the literature which, according to Bastiani (1991: 53), suggests that the way change is managed is crucial. 'Building bridges' between home and school to ease transitions represents a key factor.

However, well before a schooling choice is confirmed parents are faced with important and highly significant decisions concerning school preference. While researchers, including Petch (1986), attach importance to children's preferences, the belief in the notion of 'a caring school' and the opinions of a child's present teachers can, as Bastiani suggests (1991: 62), exert a strong influence upon parental decision-making. To assist the parents at this school, a guide entitled 'Moving on to senior school' (Booklet 7.8, p. 102) has been devised.

Towards a whole-school policy on home–school links

Wyse (reported in Bastiani, 1995) clearly articulates Moordown's approach to the development of a written policy: 'For us, it was important that the policy document should arise out of experience and practice, rather than simply be the fond hope of things to come' (51).

We see the principles underpinning the programme being the following:

- Carefully articulating the rationale underpinning this developing partnership between home and school.
- Systematically planning its work in this area, reviewing progress and redefining approaches where necessary.
- Consistently consulting with its parents through informal and formal means, actively listening to parental views and then responding in a genuine manner to show how their ideas can then influence school policy and practice.
- Continuing to improve both the range and the quality of the communication offered.
- Encouraging greater involvement in the life of our school through the creation and development of parental education programmes.
- Continuing to place at the forefront of the entire scheme the notion of *sharing expertise*, which Bastiani (1995) sees as encouraging 'a sense of shared responsibility and joint enterprise in working with parents towards their children's education and development' (53).

The importance of a home–school policy is seen as imperative, according to Sallis (1997), 'if schools are to win their [parental] support and understanding' (16). All this is encompassed within another of Moordown's parental leaflets, appropriately named 'Linking home and school' (Booklet 7.9, p. 103), which explains the school's policy.

Figure 7.14

Reading Together

Your school logo here

A helpful guide to fluent reading

---

*Sometimes children will guess and use their own clues from the text. This is <u>not</u> cheating but proves that they are reading with understanding.

*Try to find time to discuss the pictures or ask your child to predict what could happen next.

*Children should make no more than 5 to 10 errors per 100 words. Otherwise the book is likely to be inappropriate.

Extending reading

It is important for your child to realise that reading, besides being for enjoyment, can also be used for obtaining information. Children should be encouraged to read a variety of material including non-fiction, magazines, newspapers, letters and recipes to name but a few.

<u>*Remember - print isn't just to be found in books!*</u>

*Be prepared to value your child's choice of reading material and share a favourite book on more than one occasion.

*No child will continually want to read material which is challenging.

*Occasionally a reading book may not appear to be demanding or stimulating enough. Bear in mind, it may well have been chosen to consolidate recently-acquired sight vocabulary or to improve fluency, expression or heighten an awareness of spelling patterns.

*Children need constant reinforcement in all aspects of reading and language development.

Finally . . .

. . . if you would like to know more about this school's approach to reading, or have any questions specifically related to your child, please make an appointment to see the [...]

How can we help our child with reading?

This is a question countless parents ask of their child's teacher. Our booklet aims to offer practical suggestions in order to ensure your child develops and maintains a lively interest in all types of books.

Readiness for reading

Children arrive at school with a variety of pre-school experiences. Subsequently a child will only learn to read when ready to do so. Pre-reading activities can enhance a child's readiness for reading and a selection are listed below.

* Snap, Picture Lotto, Kim's Game, Odd One Out, (using letters or symbols) will all help your child to become aware of minor differences when they meet them in print - *letters like 'b', 'd' and 'p' for example.*

*Sound Lotto, taped stories and rhythms all encourage children to listen more attentively and identify and distinguish a variety of sounds.

*Joining dots from left to right and sequencing picture stories will help them to get used to the 'left-to-right sequence which reading necessitates.

*Familiarisation with phonics through 'Letterland' stories later proves essential for word-building - remember always to refer to letters by their phonic sound - ah, buh, cuh, - *rather than their name - aee, bee, cee.*

*You can help your child to record his or her own language in print by making a book using familiar pictures or photos, and writing down what they want to say about each picture.

Early reading strategies

The actual mechanics of learning to read varies from child to child. A wide selection of reading schemes and other materials allow for individual needs and preferences.

Initially your child will bring home alphabet cards followed by flash card words linked to early reading scheme books are sent home. We also offer a selection of reading games.

At a suitable stage your child will take home a reading book. Some children will make rapid progress at this stage, whilst others will progress slowly, but steadily.

We aim to use a combination of methods - word recognition, phonic skills and reading for meaning.

The Home Link Book, which accompanies the reading book, provides a record of progress and an opportunity for you and your child's teacher to make practical comments or suggestions.

Hearing your child read

Most children enjoy reading to adults because they appreciate having the undivided attention of a grown up. If they are praised for their efforts they will associate reading with pleasure.

*Never criticise your child's reading but give lavish praise for good attempts.

*If your child is very lacking in confidence, it may be helpful to read the story aloud yourself first or encourage paired reading together.

*Never pressurise your child into reading if he or she is unwilling to do so. Simply listening to the story can provide a valuable alternative.

*The flow and meaning of the text are important to sustain. Therefore, when encountering an unfamiliar word in the early stages of reading, supply the word fairly quickly, not a letter name. Alternatively, encourage word building by providing the beginning sound. However, endless 'sounding out' of words can kill reading for pleasure.

Summary

The examples throughout this chapter illustrate the point that there is clear merit in going well beyond the demands of legislation in both communicating and working with parents. Not only are they offered attractive and informed insights into the ways in which a school presents an enriching education, but also careful phraseology and the outlawing of 'edspeak' also mean that the printed matter is easily understood. The consequences are beneficial to all concerned. As Laar (1997) observes:

> apart from informing parents, it is felt that knowledge of this kind may enable and encourage them to support their children's work and contribute in ways to the planned learning activities. (328)

Underpinning all of the strategies outlined is the realisation that a home–school policy commands such importance within a school. This is because it recognises the primary educative role that parents perform. Alexander *et al.* (1995) comment that:

> schools can make a huge difference to children's lives, and if they can work more closely in partnership with parents then all our children will have a greater chance of achieving their potential. (101)

THE WELCOMING SCHOOL
How do you fare?

* **Formal contacts**

- Are prospective parents offered tours of the school?

- Are there opportunities to ask about school policy and practice?

- How are parents encouraged to help their child prepare for school?

- To what extent does the school adapt to the differing needs and perceptions of parents at the introductory meeting?

- Are there opportunities to meet the headteacher and their child's first teacher at individual interview sessions?

- Is there a framework to enable the parents to share their aspirations and concerns about their child before starting school?

- Is there a place for home visiting within the structure?

- How does the school find out what its prospective pupils know?

  From where is this information gleaned?

- To what extent does the initial meeting set the tenor for future interactions between home and school?

THE WELCOMING SCHOOL
How do you fare?

* **Those vital first impressions**

- Is the signposting to the school entrance clear and welcoming?

- What messages do parents get from their first contact with the school, whether by telephone, letter or visit?

- How attractive is the main reception?
  Does it offer somewhere comfortable to wait?
  Are there things of interest to look at?

* **Oral contact**

SCHOOL

- How are parents received.... by the office staff, headteacher, other staff and by pupils?
  Is the message a consistent one?

- With an anxious parent to what extent is reassurance given, clear information about what is happening and a genuine sense of 'being heard'?

- To what extent does the school actually 'listen' during parental exchanges?

* **Written communication**

- Is the written information always clear and understandable?

- Are enquiries always dealt with properly, whether by letter or orally?

- Are the notice boards and displays informative and inviting?

THE WELCOMING SCHOOL
How do you fare?

* **Parental perspective**

- What do existing parents say about the school's welcoming image?

- To what extent are parents satisfied with the school?

- Is the headteacher seen as approachable and helpful?

- Do parents see the teaching and support staff as approachable and sympathetic?

- To what extent are parents telling you that key members of the school's staff know their child as an individual?

- How do parents rate the school's reputation?

* **Community perspective**

- What do shopkeepers and the school's neighbours think about the school?

- How is the school rated by the local estate agents?

SCHOOL

* Make it easy to access information by including contents and an index.

* Show how learning opportunities are developed .... and the links to the next phase in the children's education.

* Keep a check on gender/ethnic bias.

* Check its format against the latest legal requirements.

* Make it interesting by including examples of children's work, illustrations and photographs.

* Think carefully about the design - an eye-catching layout speaks volumes!

* Produce it within a realistic budget.

SCHOOL

PRODUCING A SCHOOL PROSPECTUS
An aide-memoire

* Establish a production team reflecting all elements of the school community - by far the best way!

* Be clear from the outset what you want to communicate.

* Make it welcoming and user-friendly.

* Ensure it reflects your school's approach to:
  • education and the well-being of children; *and*
  • the role of parents within the home-school partnership.

* Keep it short.

* Adopt a writing style that is simple and direct. *(No jargon allowed!)*

SCHOOL

Key Stage 2.

	Autumn	Spring	Summer
Year 3	Materials	Forces	Ecology
Year 4	Human Biology	Electricity	Water
Year 5	Heating & Cooling	Light & Sound	The Environment
Year 6	The Earth in Space	Revision	Change and Growth in Humans

How can you help your children in Science . . .

* Take an interest in the Science work they do at school

* Discuss your child's progress is Science with your child's teacher at parents' evenings

* Encourage your child to play with a range of materials at home such as water

* Allow your children their own plot of garden or give them a house plant to look after

* Teach your child how to care for a pet

* Allow your child to help you with food preparation

* Encourage your child to look carefully at the world around and to ask a wide range of questions

* Take your child out for walks and encourage him or her to look carefully at what you pass

* Have a range of non-fiction books on scientific subjects available to them

* Encourage the use of a C.D. ROM encyclopaedia if you have one

* Watch scientific programmes with your children and discuss them together

* Older children might find it helpful to practice answering science questions. Many bookshops have examples of these

Written by:
Ceri Edwards-Hawthorne of Moordown St. John's CE Primary School

Science
at Moordown
St. John's

What is Science?

* At Moordown St. John's we believe that Science is the study of creation. Studying Science will help your children to make sense of the world around them and fill them with a sense of awe and wonder.

* It will also train them to think logically, solve problems, ask questions and to be more observant.

* We also hope to foster in our pupils a care for their environment.

Why do we teach Science?

* Science is a necessary part of education

* Science is a National Curriculum subject

* Science is relevant to our daily lives

* Science is exciting and enjoyable

The National Curriculum for Science

* Covers 5 areas:- nature of Science, Investigation, Biology, Chemistry and Physics.

* Says more time and importance should be given to developing children's investigative skills than in learning facts (this is because facts in Science get out of date very quickly).

* Is a core subject along with English and Mathematics.

How do we teach Science?

* At St. John's we use a wide variety of ways to teach Science and make it interesting for children.

* We usually begin our Science topics by finding out what the children already know. We often use a technique called concept mapping to do this.

* The children will then be helped to do some investigations to find out more about the topic.

Investigation Record Sheet
Use this sheet to help you plan your investigations.

Title _____ **Date** _____

Hypothesis
*This is what you think will happen and why.
I think that if ... then ..... will ... because ......
eg I think that if I add a battery to my circuit then the bulb will get brighter because there will be more power.*

Apparatus
Write here what you will use.

Method
*Use words and labelled diagrams to explain what you will do.
How will you make sure it is a fair test?
What measurements will you make?
What safety precautions will you take?*

Results
Draw a chart, table or graph or write a description to show what happened. Remember to include any units of measurement such as centimetres or minutes.

Conclusion
*Was your hypothesis correct?
What do you think now?
What further investigations would you like to try?*

What topics do the children cover?

Key Stage 1.

	Autumn	Spring	Summer
Reception	Ourselves & Materials	Forces & Materials	Living Things & Forces
Year 1	Sound / Materials	Change and Growth	Light / Materials
Year 2	Electricity and Forces	Materials	Humans & other Animals

How does it all work?

Why we report to you about your child . . .

* We see 'reporting' as part of an ongoing communication between us and you about your child.

* We believe your involvement is very significant in your child's learning.

* We pride ourselves on having open channels of communication between us and you, so that you will be encouraged and enabled to support us in educating your child.

* We have a professional responsibility and a legal requirement to keep you informed about how your child is getting on - this we do willingly.

What you can do to support our school . . .

* It is all about 'partnership' - you and us here at school working together.

* Spending time together talking ... reading ... sharing experiences ... working as well as visiting the library and places of interest ... will all help your child to grow and learn.

* Talk to us about your child's strengths, achievements and needs - this will help you to understand more about their learning.

To conclude . . .

* Your child is an individual who grows in a unique way.

* Your child's work will demonstrate their progress - celebrate it with them on a regular basis.

* Talk about your child's work . . . and support them.

* The National Curriculum tasks and tests vary from year to year and so it is not possible to accurately compare one year with another.

Remember . . .

* We are both working together to the same end, namely for the benefit of your child . . . so keep in touch!

This leaflet has been written by:
TERESA BAIN - Adviser for Assessment, Professional Development Services, Dorset County Council Educational Dept.
and HUGH WALLER - Headteacher of Moordown St. John's CE Primary School

LIFTING THE LID OFF

ASSESSMENT

Assessment is about . . .

* You and us working together to assist your child's learning.

* Talking about your child's work, identifying strengths as well as areas for improvement.

* Planning what to do next and helping your child to make progress.

* Looking at your child's work and talking with them about what they are doing.

We assess your child's progress through these ways . . .

* By looking at normal classroom work.

* By watching how he/she approaches scientific investigation.

What we do at present to inform you about your child's progress and achievement . . .

* We believe that face-to face contact and discussion is most valuable.

* We do this in two ways - formally and informally.

* Formally includes:
- an annual written report to you each July;
- termly parental consultations as follows:

AUTUMN (late September/early October): 'Meet the Teacher' ... an opportunity to get to know your child's teacher and exchange any important information at this early stage in the school year.

SPRING (March): 'An in-depth look at your child' ... looking at the progress made and recognising individual effort as well as the areas, if any, needing improvement.

SUMMER (July): 'Follow-up to the annual report' ... a chance to discuss your child's written report and share written observations for your child's next teacher.

- curriculum evenings which offer 'hands on' opportunities to learn about how and what your child is learning;

- parental information evenings about assessment ... and what it means for your child.

- special events, such as concerts, productions and presentations during acts of worship.

* Informal assessment takes the form of:
- home visits by one of our Reception teachers prior to the time when your child is due to enter school;

- brief exchanges with your child's teacher before or after school;

- home/school reading records;

- carefully-planned programmes of work to do at home.

In years 2 and 6 there are additional ways in which we assess your child . . .

* Your child will experience tasks and/or tests.
- For 7 year olds these are in English and Maths and for 11 year olds they are given in English, Maths and/or Science.

- Tasks and tests show your child's performance in selected parts of the curriculum on a particular day.

* We sum up our views about your child's progress, which we call: 'teacher assessment'; it is a judgement about what your child has achieved in a whole subject over time.

* It is in these two years that we give opportunities for you to learn more about what the 'End of Key Stage Assessments' are all about.

* Your child's summary assessments, along with the task and/or test scores are represented by 'levels' of the National Curriculum scale.

* A significant number of 7 year olds achieve 'Level 2'; we have some children scoring even higher.

* A significant number of 11 year olds achieve 'Level 4'; we even have some children scoring higher.

* It is worth remembering that at 14 (end of Key Stage 3) a significant number of children achieve 'Levels 5 or 6'.

Yr1 Autumn Term Curriculum Statement

Our topic for this term will be TOYS, with the main focus being History. We will be leading on to Victorian Toys and Victorian children. The majority of our work will be drawn from this.

How you may help

Share the enjoyment of reading through our Home Link Scheme and use the local library for the further development of enjoyment as well as for research for our Topic. Help and encourage the learning of spellings using this strategy –

LOOK at the word,
SAY the word,
COVER the word,
WRITE the word,
CHECK with the original word.

Also, ensure that your child has the appropriate amount of sleep!! Allow time each day just for a chat – this helps develop speaking skills. Lastly, encourage your child to be as independent as possible, and to take ownership of his/her own possessions and actions.

Thank you *AKBence* (MRS AK BENCE)
SJGroves (MISS SJ GROVES)

English: Speaking and Listening, Reading and Writing. There will be opportunities to share ideas, opinions, reports and describe events, listening attentively to other children and adults, asking and responding to questions and commenting on what has been said. The children will be encouraged to read a wide range of books in Year 1 both at school and at home. We will be teaching reading skills through phonics, blends, look and say, and all other methods. The children will have stories read to them and questions will be asked to test comprehension and understanding. We want to ensure that the children are reading for enjoyment – this is imperative at such an early stage. We will be using the studio for drama work linked to our Topic. There will be weekly phonetic spellings to help with unaided writing. Handwriting will be practised daily through a variety of tasks.

Mathematics: Using and Applying, Number, Shape, Space and Measures. The children will be counting, ordering and adding numbers both mentally and in written form. They will be involved in much practical work, pattern work, sorting and classifying objects and shapes as well as using the computer for problem solving games.

Science: Light and Sound. This will be taught through a variety of ways, observing, recording and exploring. Nature study will also be included in our Autumn term work on night creatures.

History: The main focus will be for the children to develop a basic sense of chronology from their life span to that of their Grandparents. This will lead on to the comparison between Victorian children and children of today, with special interest being the different toys of then and now. In order to bring this to life, we will all be actively involved in a Victorian Drama Day with Mr Simon Stone (county drama adviser). We will experience a step back in time here at school, to a Victorian classroom and the Victorian method of teaching, wearing Victorian clothes and looking at and using Victorian toys. This will be on Tuesday October 14th, more details will follow early in the term.

RE: Biblical stories linked to the family and children; Moses and Joseph. We will look at the giving and receiving of presents within the Christmas story.

PSE: To encourage equal relationships between everyone and to encourage the children to talk about personal and social issues within the security of our class group.

Health: Looking after ourselves and the importance of good manners and following our School Code.

Art, Craft & Design: The children will be given many opportunities to experience a wide range of Art through using different media. They will be taught a variety of skills and work in a small group with an adult.

Design & Technology: The children will work co-operatively to develop their D & T skills in making a class Toy Shop. They will be looking at the quality of a great variety of Toys and will have the opportunity to design and make a toy from a wide range of materials.

IT: The children will initially work in pairs through the 'My World' programme which involves problem solving and requires the children to develop and use basic computer skills.

PE: Gymnastics, Dance and Swimming skills will be developed during this term.

Yr4 Autumn Term
Curriculum Statement

How you may help

* Help and encourage with weekly spellings.

* Help and encourage with weekly multiplication tables.

* Encourage visits to Library to select fiction and information books.

* Children may be asked to research specific areas of projects, maths or Topical news so your co-operation with these tasks would be appreciated.

Our topic for this term will be the Ancient Greeks and much of our work will be drawn from this theme.

Year 4 Autumn Term
Curriculum Statement

Our topic for this term will be the Ancient Greeks and much of our work will be drawn from this theme.

English: Speaking and Listening, Reading and Writing

There will be opportunities to share ideas, opinions, reports and describe events. Children will be encouraged to listen attentively to other children and adults asking and responding to questions and commenting on what has been said. Children will gain confidence as speakers and listeners in small group and whole class activities including drama. They will read a wide range of fiction and non-fiction individually and in group reading and will be introduced to research skills. Children will have experience of writing for a variety of emphasis with developing emphasis on grammar, spelling and handwriting.

Mathematics:
Using and Applying Maths, Number, Shape, Space and Measures

The revision and extension of number skills in addition, subtraction and multiplication are to be undertaken using mental mathematics and tables to reinforce concepts. Children will be encouraged in the development of their presentational skills. Problem solving, investigations, estimations and approximations will be included where appropriate. There will be an emphasis on angles, shapes and nets together with linear measurements.

Science: Life and Life Processes

Children to develop some understanding of the human body, included in this study will be: teeth, dental care, types of food and its importance to growth, exercise and health. Children to develop an understanding of main organs in the body and how they work, respiration, the skeleton and the importance of exercise and rest.

History

Ancient Greece, myths and legends, life in Athens and Sparta, architecture and art, Persian wars and the influence of the ancient Greek culture on the rest of the world.

Geography

To identify Britain on the map and the location of Greece in the Mediterranean and compare with the location of the ancient Greek empire.

Religious Education

Link with Greek heroes and modern examples of heroes that will include Jewish heroes, Christian Saints. We will be looking at the Fathers and prophets of the Jewish faith as well as Christian examples.

Art

Children will improve and develop the practical skills needed to make artefacts including modelling, sewing, painting and clay work.

Technology

Design and make a Greek Temple.

Information Technology

Develop word processing skills and manipulate text. Collect, construct and enter data into a data base.

Music

Distinguish between steps, leaps and repeats in melodies and types of movement.
Identify and distinguish between long and short phrases.
Identify different metres and respond through movement.
Identify rhythm patterns aurally.
Make sounds/ instruments for specific effects.

Physical Education

The children will be encouraged to develop movement, gymnastic, swimming and ball games skills.

Ways we encourage learning

- Giving verbal and non-verbal praise.

- Displaying work for others to see.

- Writing helpful and encouraging comments.

- Providing lots of different incentives:
  - stickers and badges (infants)
  - stars and team points (juniors)

- Special efforts receive recognition:
  - 'Golden Apple' award (infants)
  - 'Headteacher Award' stickers
  - printed certificates
  - congratulatory letter.

If work is not finished ... what then?

- We always give a child the chance to complete work that is not done by using playtimes.

- If this often happens then the teacher speaks with the child's parents.

- Our teachers strike a balance about pursuing work not handed in, since we do not want this to detract from teaching the other children in the class.

- However, please remember that the activities we set in our home study programme are always useful and relevant. We hope children feel they want to complete them.

We review our home study programme regularly .....

This we achieve by:
- everyone observing it in action and seeing if it is working effectively.

- receiving comments, favourable or otherwise, from our school's teaching staff, the parents and members of the Governing Body.

- holding regular feedback sessions among the teaching staff.

- making changes, where necessary, that have the children's best interests uppermost.

Help is always available

- The teaching staff are ready and willing to provide assistance; remember to make an appointment if you want some time with your child's teacher.

- We invite you to attend one of the regular workshop sessions for parents. Not only do we share our home study programme with you but we also suggest how this can help your child learn more effectively.

Some final points ....

- If your child is off school because of illness we assume that he or she is not well enough to work.

- If your child is away for some time but can work at home then we can provide this.

- Where family holidays are taken in term time we feel they should be enjoyed. If parents so wish their child(ren) can prepare an illustrated diary.

'From little acorns mighty oaks trees grow.'

Our Home Study Programme

Important first principles

- Links between home and school are important to us.

- 'Working together' ensures that the children are offered the best education.

- This school believes it is important that children bring 'work' home from a young age.

- In recognising this, we give our home study programme a special title ...

- Starting in the Reception Year enables parents to help their child to learn.

- Children need to see their parents and this school working together.

- Home study times need to be short and regular with the emphasis on 'daily' as children get older.

- At all times activities are chosen to engage the children's interest.

- Through our home study programme we want to broaden the children's thinking and reasoning skills so they become more effective learners.

- Most importantly, for this programme to work well it must always have the fullest support of parents.

How much work at home?

- 'Little and often' ... is our motto with the younger children.

- The amount of work increases as the children get older.

- More precise information appears in the year group curriculum statements, which parents receive on a regular basis.

- Also, as the children get older, we encourage them to take a growing responsibility for their learning. Working together as a family is important from the outset.

The best time and place ...

- Let children 'unwind' first as they will have been busy and worked hard at school.

- Don't choose a time when it is your child's favourite television programme.

- With younger children find somewhere cosy and comfortable to do things together.

- For older children provide a room without distractions which has a sizeable worktop space.

- Try to reach a compromise about the best time for study so that other interesting and exciting things can be done too.

What is given for home study activities

- This varies according to the age of the child.

- Again, more details appear in the year group information statements.

- As children get older so the work programme builds on earlier learning at school and at home.

Ways parents can help

- 'Work together' with this school.

- Ensure that work done by your child is always their best.

- Provide the best place at home for work to be done ... well!

- Agree a work routine with your child which suits everyone.

- Encourage your child to work at their own pace.

- Give plenty of praise - this will encourage your child to remain enthusiastic about their work.

- Allow your child to pursue their own interests and outside activities.

- Check to see that your child is not spending excessive amounts of time on a particular task or might be getting distressed.

- If there are ever any concerns or problems, however small, then contact your child's teacher as soon as possible - don't forget!

Yes ... computers can be used

- There are times when this is a good idea.

- If your child has access to word processing or data handling facilities then we encourage their use.

- However, don't worry if this equipment is not available in your home - your child will not be disadvantaged.

What we look for in our LSAs

In choosing LSAs this school is wanting to recruit people who:

* want to work together as a team with all other members of our school staff.

* treat every one equally and fairly.

* always set a good example to others.

* actively praise and encourage good behaviour in children, acting appropriately whenever misbehaviour is seen.

* fully endorse 'Our School Code'.

* always display the right attitude to the job.

* patrol their area regularly.

* demonstrate a responsibility for health and safety and see that it is promoted.

* are aware of the school surroundings and any potential dangers to others.

* will challenge politely any 'strangers' seen and escort them to the School Office or senior member of staff.

* will act sensibly and calmly during any emergency situation.

* can deal with incidents efficiently and effectively...knowing who to tell and when.

* will observe our stated practices when dealing with children needing first aid.

* ensure that all confidential information is treated as such.

* see the importance of regular training as a way of doing the job even better.

Regular training for our LSAs

* Our school sees this as a very important reinforcement of our LSAs' duties.

* Our school policy on 'Lunchtime Supervision' provides our LSAs with a written record of what to do.

* The regular meetings enable us to deal with any operational problems and to look to ways of improving practice.

Our team of Lunchtime Supervisory Assistants (LSAs)...

Their names are:

Selecting new LSAs

* If interested in being considered for a LSA position then please speak with our School Office staff.

* All permanent posts are advertised in the local newspaper.

© 1997 Moordown St. John's CE Primary School, Bournemouth.

Place your school logo here

LUNCHTIME SUPERVISION

Supervision at lunchtimes

* During lunchtimes the children are looked after by a team of Lunchtime Supervisory Assistants (LSAs).

* Overseeing the LSAs is a duty senior supervisor, who is a member of our school's senior management.

* In the Autumn Term we have ...... LSAs. As our young Reception children become full-time, so we have more male and female LSAs.

* Whenever our LSAs cannot do lunchtime duties we try to get an approved replacement from our 'reserve list'.

What we expect of the children

* Through the lunchtime period the children are expected to co-operate with our LSAs in the same way they would with any of the teachers.

What our LSAs do

* Each Infant LSA looks after one class, whilst the children eat their packed meal. After this the LSAs supervise these young children playing outside.

* Our team of Junior LSAs rotate between supervising the children eating their lunches in the Hall and overseeing outdoor play.

* At mealtimes our LSAs ensure the children:
- wash their hands beforehand
- display good table manners
- leave their table tidy.

* In the summer months the children eat outside in supervised groups.

* Outside our LSAs ensure the children are - suitably dressed
- play sensibly in the playground
- are not left on their own unless
- through choice.

* Some of our LSAs are qualified first aiders, offering full cover throughout the lunchtime period.

Promoting positive behaviour

* Our LSAs are always looking for times to praise and encourage children who are well-behaved.

* This links with 'Our School Code'............

* You will understand we want children to play and act fairly towards each other.

Our School Code
1. We try to be followers of Jesus in everything we do and say.
2. We are polite, kind and helpful to everyone.
3. We know it is important to listen to others.
4. We walk quietly around our school.
5. We look after all that is in our school.
6. We respect and care for one another.

* Our LSAs encourage this by:
- *giving praise*
- *sharing a child's achievements with others*
- *recommending children for award stickers (infant/juniors) and team points (juniors).*

* Our team of LSAs will also use any of the following sanctions whenever a child, or group of children, is not well-behaved:
- *waiting until after the normal starting time before being allowed to eat their lunch*
- *being required to eat alone*
- *separating one or more from their friends*
- *staying with the LSA instead of enjoying free play*
- *having misused or inappropriate playthings confiscated.*

* Whenever there is an incident of very bad behaviour then one of the school's senior management is immediately involved... and the parents too.

Knowledge and Understanding of the World

The children are learning to:

* talk about:
  - where they live
  - the neighbourhood
  - their families
  - past and present events in their lives

* recognise and pick out features of living things, objects and events

* say what things are for in their neighbourhood

* talk about their observations

* record what they see

* ask questions to gain further information

* display these skills
  (e.g. cutting, joining, folding and building) using them in subjects like technology

Physical Development

The children are learning to:

* move confidently
  ... and with imagination, when required

* display increasing control and co-ordination

* show an awareness of space
  ... and of others around them

* use a range of small and large equipment, as well as the climbing and balancing apparatus with increasing skill

* handle appropriate tools, objects, construction and malleable materials safely ... and with increasing control

Creative Development

The children are learning to:

* explore sound and colour, texture, shape and form, as well as space (2D and 3D)

* respond in a variety of ways to what they see, hear, smell, touch and feel

* increasingly use their imagination in adaptable ways to listen and observe ... through art, music, dance, stories and imaginative play

* express their ideas and communicate their feelings using a widening range of materials, suitable tools, instruments and other resources

Desirable Outcomes for Children's Learning

Personal and Social Development

Language and Literacy

Mathematics

Knowledge and Understanding of the World

Physical Development

Creative Development

Personal and Social Development

The children are learning to:

* display a growing confidence

* get on well with other children and adults

* work happily together and on their own

* show sensitivity and respect for others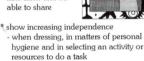

* ask for help if it is needed

* take turns and be able to share

* show increasing independence
  - when dressing, in matters of personal hygiene and in selecting an activity or resources to do a task

* display an eagerness to learn

* behave appropriately

* be increasingly aware of 'right' and 'wrong'

* treat things around them with care

* show a range of feelings - wonder, joy and sorrow

* grow in their faith as followers of Jesus (linked more closely to RE and School Worship)

Language and Literacy

The children are learning to:

* listen attentively

* talk about their experiences

* express themselves using a growing vocabulary and with increasing fluency

* listen and respond to stories, nursery rhymes and poems

* make up their own stories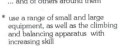

* take part in role play situations

* enjoy books and understand how they are organised, including how to handle them carefully

* know about the simple conventions of English

* start associating sounds with patterns in rhymes

* use pictures, symbols, familiar words and letters to communicate meaning

* begin to be aware of the different purposes of writing

* recognise their own name and some familiar words

* write their own name correctly using upper and lower case letters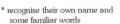

Mathematics

The children are learning to:

* use simple mathematical language
  - such as circle, in front of, bigger than ...

* pick out patterns and to create them, too

* use, with increasing confidence, their developing mathematical understanding to solve practical problems

* compare, sort, match, order sequence and count using everyday objects

* recognise and use numbers to 10

* show familiarity with larger numbers from their everyday lives

* begin to show an awareness of certain number operations within a practical context and the language involved, too - in addition and

If there are any further
questions regarding
the particular suitability
of a senior school for
your child please do
not hesitate to contact ...

* Hugh Waller (Headteacher)
* Year 6 teachers

at this present school. We shall be only too
pleased to offer whatever assistance we can.

MOVING ON TO SENIOR SCHOOL

MOVING ON TO SENIOR SCHOOL

To start with...

* be clear about the choices of senior school available to you.
* try to make preliminary visits to your preferred choice of schools.

Things for you to bear in mind

1. How close is the senior school to our home?
2. Does an elder brother and/or sister already attend the school?
3. How important is it for our child to be at the same school as their friends?

Undertake a preliminary visit

* Have regard for your <u>first impressions</u> of the feel, layout of the school and general orderliness of the pupils.

- look for evidence of pupils' work and school activities in displays around the school.
- enquire about the sizes of classes and how pupils are grouped.
- observe the quality of the facilities offered (for example, in science, technology, creative and expressive arts (music, art and design, dance, drama), information technology and sports.
- enquire about the choices of GCSE subjects offered and whether timetabling prevents certain subjects from being taken alongside one another.

* Request a copy of the <u>School Prospectus</u> which should provide you with information.

- Policies on
  * discipline
  * homework
  * learning support
  * able pupils
  * assessment
  * reward and achievement.

- In addition you want to know about the opportunities for:

  * career guidance
  * work experience
  * links with industry, business and commerce.

* Use every opportunity to speak with the school's headteacher, the staff *and* the pupils.

Consider your child's strengths and interests

* Bear in mind any particular strength, interest and ability your child may have.

* You may wish to enquire about the facilities or opportunities provided in the areas of music, sport, drama and the creative and expressive arts in general.

What kind of involvement does the school have with its parents?

- opportunities for consultation about pupil progress
- assessment of work and reporting to parents
- PTA meetings - procedure for dealing with concerns and/or complaints
- opportunities for parents to assist in school
- ways parents can help at home in supporting their child's learning.

Last, but not least, take account of the overall ethos of the senior school

* Does the school appear to be a caring community which praises and encourages achievement of any kind, whether academic or otherwise?

Your child's progress

* So that parents can maintain a fully active role in their child's education we undertake to keep everyone fully informed by circulating year group study programmes.

* Whilst our school holds termly parental consultations, parents can meet with their child's teacher at other times - this is usually by appointment so that sufficient time is given for the exchange.

* This school prides itself on clear, readable and well-presented annual written reports. These appear around the beginning of July each year.

Keeping you informed

Watch out for our regular newsletters... and publicity posters.

Our Parents and Friends Association (PFA) and Governing Body also produce termly newsletters and annual reports.

Our commitment

* Our practice of *'SHARING EXPERTISE'* is built around *'confidence, co-operation and communication'*.

* We continually monitor the success of our home-links. We do this by canvassing parental, staff and governor opinion, generally using questionnaires.

Points of contact

* If you wish to raise a matter or concern about our home-school link programme then please contact:
HUGH WALLER (Headteacher)
or
SYBIL WYATT (Chairman of Governors).

* Both people may be contacted via the school:
Telephone: 01202 527683 or
Facsimile: 01202 513877

'LINKING HOME AND SCHOOL'

First principles

* At our school we are eager to establish good and effective working relationships between home and school.

* To this end we see it as important for us to:
... *make every parent feel welcome.*

... *keep parents fully informed about their child and about school activities.*

... *always listen to our parents as this is a most powerful way of communicating.*

... *look to ways of breaking down any barriers so helping parents to feel 'at home' in and around the school.*

... *involve parents in all decision-making processes.*

... *encourage parents to use their own skills to help their child at home.*

Ways we encourage our home-school links

* Even from the point of initially registering a child's name parents are given every chance to see this school *'in action'*.

* We offer a comprehensive pre-school preparation programme to all children gaining a place here. We are very eager to offer each child *'a very good start'*.

* A starting school profile, called *'Early Milestones'*, is provided for the parents and their child to complete. We are eager to learn from parents about their pre-school child.

* We provide regular written communications in ways that interest our readership.

* Meetings at school are taken seriously; staff are available ... and ready to listen.

* We welcome help from parents in many and different ways. We even offer training, too, for those helping in classrooms and in undertaking reprographics work.

* Membership of our Parents and Friends Association is actively encouraged.

Sharing our practice

* We acknowledge that parents play a vital role in supporting their child's education.

* Ways are pursued, normally through activity workshops, to develop parental understanding of our school curriculum.

* We do this so that parents can help their child as much as possible.

* New and different parental workshops are continuing to appear. So watch this space!

8   Evaluating recent initiatives in promoting home–school links

An overview

The Labour government elected in May 1997 is, like all other political parties, committed to strengthening relationships between parents and their children's schools.

'Accountability' is now a feature of partnership initiatives, whether we like it or not. One might argue that the notion of 'enforcement' runs counter to the creativity and spontaneity that manifests itself in the initiatives explored so far. The teaching profession, well used to imposed change, will no doubt harness these politically driven directives. Comment is offered in this chapter as to ways in which this might occur, focusing on a number of current initiatives. We would argue that individual school communities and local education authorities should, wherever possible, retain the right of 'ownership'.

Baseline assessment – the proposals

From 1998 primary schools will have to assess reception pupils according to certain guidelines. At the time of going to print the educational world has been awaiting the definitive 'Baseline Assessment Scales' (1997) produced by the School Curriculum and Assessment Authority (SCAA), which are the consequence of trialling and exhaustive consultation during 1996–7.

The national framework produced by SCAA, now known as the Qualifications and Curriculum Authority (QCA), requires that a baseline assessment scheme should:

1. Appropriately assess all children.
2. Identify children's special educational learning needs and provide for effective teacher planning.
3. Enable later progress to be monitored and contribute to the 'value-added' factor.
4. Involve parents in the assessment process.
5. Take place in the first seven weeks of entry into the reception class.
6. Focus upon desirable outcomes in key areas.
7. Be undertaken in an unobtrusive way as part of the child's daily routine.
8. Not be too burdensome for teachers.
9. Form a part of the child's record of achievement and the school's assessment policy, and build on comments and assessments from preschool providers and parents.

In order for relative pupil progress, or the 'value-added' factor, to be measured, it was deemed necessary for children's knowledge and skills to be measured in a consistent way. This meant a numerical score had to be provided by both the baseline assessment and later by the end of Key Stage assessment tests. SCAA have decided to accredit schemes by judging them against the criteria in the national framework and to publish a list of accredited schemes annually. These must be appropriate for use in more than one school.

Initial reactions

Wolfendale (1993b) acknowledges that some form of on-entry assessment is educationally desirable. However, she believes that 'the "best interests" of children [should] be paramount, at all times' (40). From various INSET conferences with which Wolfendale had been involved, she found a consensus amongst head teachers and early years teachers that they did not wish to have a baseline assessment prescribed for them. They wanted to decide upon the most appropriate system which, as she sums it up should be a 'confirmation, affirmation [and] celebration of development and attainment to date' (41). However, this would not highlight the discrepancy between the various expectations of reception class teachers regarding their pupils during the first year in school.

There is a body of opinion, in part expressed by parents, that some children are being denied early access to some areas of the curriculum. Baseline assessment, in its present guise, may help to ensure that each child has the best possible start, knowing that teachers are likely to plan their curriculum so that children will achieve well in the tests.

However, Merttens (1992) is disturbed by the idea of a profile of a child's achievements upon entry to school, as she feels low attainment implies poor parenting, 'the end result of the widespread use of such records could be to define what it is to be a *good* or *bad* parent' (16). Is there a danger in using a child's performance to measure their parent's success?

Parental opinion has also been sought in a qualitative way. Maxwell and Hofkins (1996) recount the outcome of parental interviews commissioned by the *Times Educational Supplement*. While most of them favoured baseline assessment in principle, seeing that it would assist schools with differing intakes to chart pupil progress, they were 'concerned about children being labelled as less intelligent because they are younger than average when starting school or have been less well prepared by their parents or in preschool' (12). The consensus view was that the tests would be too hard for a child who had just reached the age of four, yet would have been acceptable for a child approaching five years of age.

The TES survey also highlighted parental concern about the baseline assessment's failure to recognise the significance of social skills, such as behaviour, making friends, listening and talking. These the parents see as equating in importance to the three Rs. Furthermore, the notion of 'ticking boxes' to record a child's development is dismissed. Rather parents are prepared to accept the reception teachers' professionalism in judging the attainment of these young children through observation and conversation.

Two common trends emerge from this survey. The first is an overwhelming parental desire to receive guidelines outlining what children should be able to achieve upon entry. SCAA's response, as reported to the TES, was that it.

> planned to provide information for parents about reasonable expectations for children on starting school. But they recognise it is hard to generalise, particularly as children start school at different ages. (Maxwell and Hofkins 1996)

Secondly, there remains a scepticism about how the baseline assessment framework will demonstrate 'value added' within primary schools. This is, in part, fuelled by the belief that some schools may be tempted to under-estimate children's skills deliberately in order that the school's 'value-added' element may appear greater.

Interestingly, a MORI survey undertaken by SCAA has confirmed that, contrary to the Authority's belief, parents do not wish to be involved in the assessment process. The view is that 'they might not be as objective as the teacher. They would bring their own views of wanting their children to do well' (Maxwell and Hofkins 1996). However, there is an overwhelming parental desire to receive a report on the outcome of their child's assessment.

Contracts and agreements – which way forward?

As a key educational issue, the recently elected Labour government views home–school contracts as a *fait accompli* for all schools. Blunkett (reported in Bastiani 1996) states that 'Labour will introduce a home–school contract to build a stronger partnership between every teacher and parent' (12). Fortunately, it has been decided to defer making the award of a school place dependent on the signing of a home–school contract.

It is too soon to imagine that contracts or agreements immediately resolve the many intractable problems facing some schools. Nevertheless, successful initiatives are happening in localised parts of the country, as reported by Bastiani (1996: 25–33), and therefore the principle should not be wholly decried.

Our argument stems from this notion of 'imposition'. We see this clearly undermining the 'shared understanding' forged locally, whether at local education authority level or by one or more schools, from which a home–school policy naturally evolves. Most parents wish to support their child at school but they are looking for 'partnership', not 'power'. As Tulloch (1997) states, 'signing a bit of paper will not turn them into partners ... the imposition of contracts is more likely to lead to division than partnership' (23). And what of the family that temporarily faces particularly difficult domestic circumstances? This would place a strain on the contract commitment they have made, thus leaving them with a sense of guilt and failure.

The Campaign for State Education (1996) makes the valid point that it is a policy, not a contract, that brings about whole-school commitment:

> to encourage school and home to work together to support the children's learning ... [being] ... shared, supported and understood by parents, teachers and governors, not a legalistic contract which parents have to sign.

Sallis (1997), writing in the *Times Educational Supplement*, concurs with this viewpoint by stating that

> the partnerships which really work are between those who enter them freely and as equal partners ... the winning of parents' trust requires respect, patience and understanding, not blame. (16)

Such an approach brings with it effective parental empowerment and genuine cooperation between home and school, coupled with an increased support for children's learning. Our school practice mirrors this message – imposing contracts or agreements will damage the creative partnerships that exist.

Record of Achievement

The title 'Record of Achievement' itself acts as a prompt to bear in mind that the emphasis should always remain on the child's *achievement* and should not be a checklist which highlights failure.

Neal *et al.* (1990) offer a synopsis of their development:

> Records of Achievement were originally piloted in secondary schools. In 1985 nine pilot schemes, covering 22 LEAs and some 250 schools, were established. These schemes were funded by an Education Support Grant and reported to a National Records of Achievement Steering Committee (RANSC). This Committee published a report on the pilot work in 1989. In this, it recommended that Records of Achievement should be developed in primary schools and throughout the five to sixteen range. (2)

The Government's baseline assessment framework offers parents the opportunity to participate in the assessment process upon entry. It recognises the valuable information parents are able to offer about their child. Children can only benefit when they see parents and teachers working together in a mutually supportive role. An atmosphere of mutual trust will ensure each side tries to do its best for the child. Schools must acknowledge parents as the child's primary educators and, as such, they should continue to be involved in an advisory and complementary capacity.

Records of Achievement can prove valuable for the following reasons:

- They provide continuity from class to class, informing subsequent teachers of a child's progress.
- They give an all-round picture of the child, not only a record of academic achievement.
- Parents are involved in the assessment and recording process.
- National Curriculum levels achieved can be recorded in a simple way.

Records of Achievement for Key Stage 1

We have drawn up a Record of Achievement suitable for use with the four- to seven-year age group. Contributions are added to the Record of Achievement even prior to the child starting school, and it culminates with the final report at the end of Key Stage 1. Although the Record of

Achievement ultimately belongs to the child it remains in the school until the end of that key stage.

Our Record of Achievement consists of a set of photocopiable masters which are provided in plastic pockets in order to protect them from damage. When photocopied they can be placed in a ring-bound file.

The pack consists of:

- An initial profile of the preschool child entitled 'Introducing Me'
  (there will be space for a personal photograph, details of health, home–school visits and previous preschool experience);
- Yearly sheets called 'More about Me' which act as a self-assessment and give an updated insight into the child's personality
  (this section allows for comments on interests, successes, friendships, likes and dislikes);
- A joint sheet for parent and child to complete each year entitled 'Getting to know Me out of School'
  (photocopies of certificates and photographs of special events can be included here);
- A sheet for the teacher to complete when reporting on the teacher/child twice-yearly review of performance;
- Assessment sheets, completed annually, relating to the National Curriculum and carried out informally within the child's normal daily routine
  (samples of work and/or photographic evidence can be used to show the extent of progress);
- A set of activity sheets to support the National Curriculum tasks
  (schools should add the baseline assessment results, the yearly written reports and the end of Key Stage 1 assessment results).

Experience convinces us that the majority of parents wish to be involved in their child's education. A Record of Achievement is evidence of the school's concern to keep the parents both involved and informed about their child's progress. They are given the opportunity to participate in decision-making and their strengths and expertise are recognised and valued. Children's comments are invited to give them a feeling of involvement in the process of their own learning.

Sample sheets from the Record of Achievement appear in Figure 8.1 (p. 108). The complete packs are obtainable from Primary Headstart Publications.

Accredited status for parent learning

Set against an agenda whereby parent education is achieving greater status through the development of courses both locally and nationally, the accreditation of parent learning represents an interesting dimension. Bastiani (1995), in reporting on the 'Parents in a Learning Society' project (1993–5) sponsored by the Royal Society for the Encouragement of Arts, Manufactures and Commerce (RSA), recounts how this has been pioneered in several schools.

While not directly influenced by the RSA initiative, this school has, over the past five years, been evolving its own, successful parent education programme. This is due to several factors, among them:

1. The advanced stage reached in the realisation of an effective partnership with parents.
2. The welcoming ethos of the school, characterised, according to Bastiani (1995), 'by informal, friendly relationships with its parents' (37).
3. The accessibility of a deliberately structured course, even though it requires a defined, prior commitment on the part of each participant.
4. The training programme's appeal in focusing upon parents' roles as educators.
5. The relaxed, informal structure of the course in encouraging active involvement by each of the participants.
6. Having successfully completed the four-evening course, the recognition of parental achievement in the form of a signed certificate (Fig. 8.2, p. 109).

However, the longer-term consequence of providing successful in-school training for parents is

Figure 8.1 (2)

Figure 8.1 (1)

Figure 8.2

that it unleashes unstoppable energies. Acting as a catalyst, it has empowered a number of individuals by giving them renewed confidence to undertake educational careers in new and exciting directions. The enlisting of replacement volunteers by the new entrants – seen as an occupational hazard – ensures that the school-based demand is largely satisfied. Furthermore, the course has also generated a more questioning audience which some may view as a threat – it requires the staff to be well prepared!

The course is planned and delivered by an external literacy consultant with many years experience as a classroom practitioner. Entitled 'Helping in School', it offers parents support before they begin. The training has been planned to develop awareness and a perception of the volunteer role about to be undertaken. By examining various elements of the role it is possible to deal more effectively with them. Five areas are considered, namely:

- *Perception*
- *Learning*
- *Behaviour control*
- *Literacy skills*
- *Confidence and stress.*

Further details regarding the content appear in the guidance notes (Fig. 8.3, p. 110–11).

By making the learning explicit, we would argue that the programme outlined is easily transferable to other school situations. Subsequently the level of volunteer support this school enjoys is currently in excess of 120 people per week!

From the school's perspective, the relaxed atmosphere permits course members to ask questions and to share their knowledge. Use is made of published videos where they support the learning focus. Furthermore, the course helps to demonstrate to parents the depth of the volunteer role, thereby providing them with the chance to reconsider if they wish. Conversely, the school is given the opportunity to review the suitability of the parents in a positive manner as not all are suited to the work involved. As the course presenter, Maureen Mills, declares, 'we consider that parents have much to offer. The course is intended to help them to help the school. We appreciate their help and trust that the course demonstrates our appreciation.'

Figure 8.3 (1)

PARENT HELPERS' TRAINING COURSE
Guidance notes

Introduction

* Stress school's belief in good parent-school relationships and how it values parental contribution inside and out of the classroom.
* Parents, teachers and children working in harmony represent the most important resource for any school; however, not achieved without political will and hard work.
* Outline pattern of parents working as voluntary classroom assistants.
* School's policy to offer support and training beforehand.
* Training focuses upon developing awareness and perception of role about to be undertaken; by so doing, deal more efficiently with it.

'Perception'

* Once extra person introduced into classroom, group dynamics immediately altered; teacher, helper and children all have expectations.
* Unless time taken to plan role of classroom helper, confusion will arise which leads to misunderstandings and division.
* Importance of social implications - classroom helper must be discreet; not always easy because have more intimate role in society which school serves, and opportunities to be drawn into discussions about school policies and personnel are greater.
* Helpers are not teachers, yet are privy to more than the visiting parent, so their situation is particular - important to be aware of this.
* Important to be sensitive to feelings of other parents of children attending the school - if child having difficulty with school work, parents do not wish this to become common knowledge, are nervous of parent helpers becoming involved and being indiscreet; some feel their help is inappropriate.
* Important to demonstrate the support element in helper role; certainly not intention of course to suggest visiting parents take over role of the teachers!
* Consider teacher's perception of the role and expectations; necessary that time shared so classroom helper aware of these - can vary between classrooms.
* Never easy to know how involved to be - too much becomes 'pushy'; not enough seen as as 'ineffectual'.
* Children see classroom assistant as different from the teacher - act appropriately, possibly becoming too familiar or too noisy in that person's company; has to be dealt with immediately with adults discussing beforehand their various roles in maintaining discipline.
* Teachers have different ways of working (not better or worse); important for classroom assistant to work within these parameters.
* Include group discussion and role-play to highlight some of these social implications and avoid possible conflict.

'Learning'

* Support of ancillary helpers is of proven worth; quality of their intervention enhanced as their understanding of learning process extended.
* Explore how children learn by looking at two aspects of learning behaviour.
* Firstly we look at strengths individuals bring to the learning process (e.g. visual and auditory perception, all aspects of memory, language usage and sequencing skills).
* To identify elements we bring to learning, pursue activities whereby group uses short-term memory, visual and auditory recall and is required to respond visually and orally to present information; demonstrates we all learn in different ways, explains why teachers need to present work in variety of formats, need for individual strategies since what works for one will not work for all!
* Then explore teaching strategies and processes - e.g. individual programmes, group work, rote learning, music, drama, etc. - used by teachers to provide appropriate learning experiences for their pupils.
* By end of this module expect group to have identified a number of important points - that we all learn in different ways; that we tend to teach the way we learn because we perceive this as the most productive strategy; that we need to share knowledge to acquire a fund of strategies to offer children; that we need to be flexible and offer as many varied learning opportunities as we can think of to facilitate learning; also no matter how we present the next stage in learning, unless previous work has been understood we will not be successful.

Figure 8.3 (2)

PARENT HELPER TRAINING COURSE
Guidance notes (continued)

'Behaviour Control'

* When discussing behaviour always assumed we mean bad behaviour; not so! Children need to be encouraged to behave appropriately.
* Course includes input on appropriate behaviour; consider variety of modes of behaviour which can inhibit learning.
* Because classroom assistant is perceived differently by the children and as they frequently work with them in small groups or individually, methods of altering inappropriate behaviour can be subtle and more intimate.
* Needs to be pointed out that if the adult changes his/her behaviour then this results in a change in the child's behaviour.
* Inappropriate adult behaviour, like sarcasm and ridicule, is addressed.
* Explore the impact of tone of voice and body language; through small group work consider possible tactics to change behaviour and then share these with the whole group for evaluation.

'Literacy Skills'

* Many classroom helpers find themselves closely involved with children who have weak reading skills and have difficulty expressing themselves on paper.
* Because it is commonly thought that all such problems stem directly from some malfunction within the child we look at what is meant by 'dyslexia'.
* Group has opportunity to peruse and discuss current tests to ascertain if a child is dyslexic; through general discussion establish notion that it is difficult for untrained person to identify the dyslexic child.
* Group made aware of problems peculiar to the dyslexic child and how to help.
* Taking this further, group then looks at how reading has been taught historically and how lack of flexibility and rigid adherence to any single method can be beneficial to some but less so for others.
* By means of group activity consider strategies we bring to reading.
* Also look at ways of listening to children read, with strong emphasis being placed on 'paired reading' and a game approach to developing sight vocabulary.
* To help a child create text consider how to support spelling and extend these skills; following strategies explored - individual dictionaries, collective resources for classroom, ways of offering spelling to children (e.g. child to make an attempt which is then checked, effort praised and altered where necessary).
* Course members encouraged to make own games and share them; also use computer games (popular with children).
* Finally, look at ways of encouraging story-telling since if a child cannot tell a story then (s)he cannot write one; course members encouraged to share successful ways (e.g. group story at an oral level which is scribed by the teacher and then used as a reading resource; story can be scribed by the teacher, then sentences cut into strips and re-arranged by the children).
* Explore techniques to encourage writing (e.g. using sequence of pictures to support the text, re-organising text, cloze procedure, brain-storming, etc.)
* Important to stress that although value of these strategies are well known to teachers they are not always understood by helpers.

'Confidence and Stress'

* Important for those working with children to understand significance of self-confidence; most important gift a parent helper can give is a good perception of him/herself.
* Group considers ways to improve and develop confidence in children and how this can be inadvertently destroyed.
* Consider value of praise and how to praise a child who is having difficulty producing work worthy of praise.
* Emphasise that in all things school policy on behaviour management must be understood and adhered to.
* No matter how we feel a situation should have been handled, any discussion arising should be with the teacher and not the child!

The authors acknowledge with gratitude this written contribution from Maureen Mills, who leads the Parent Helper Training courses at Moordown St John's CE Primary School.

Furthermore, examining this initiative from the partnership perspective, Laar (1997) observes that it 'can be particularly valuable in that it enlarges the possibility of extended interaction between the teacher and groups of pupils' (328–9).

Reviewing performance

Complementing the various external audit approaches which have been explored in Chapter 6, schools are now witnessing a resurgence of interest in 'self-evaluation'. Focusing upon these questions – *What constitutes success?* and *How can success be measured?* – we would suggest that they are not simply the province of a school's senior management. Rather they are the business of everyone on the staff working in partnership with the school governors. It is important that a school's 'home–school links' are included within this spotlight. Research (for example, Mortimer *et al.* 1988) suggests that partnership with parents represents a key component in measuring the success of a school.

Not wishing to re-invent the wheel, a study commissioned by the National Union of Teachers (MacBeath *et al.* 1996) has highlighted a range of success indicators, a few of which are directly applicable to assessing the effectiveness of parental partnership within a school setting (Fig. 8.4). Very helpful qualitative and quantitative pointers are offered along with methodological approaches to gathering the evidence. If used appropriately these indicators enable a school to establish specific goals for management. It is time well spent!

Figure 8.4

INDICATING 'SUCCESS' IN HOME-SCHOOL PARTNERSHIPS

* **School climate**
  - school is a safe and happy place
  - school is welcoming to visitors and newcomers

* **Relationships**
  - parents...feel welcomed and valued in the school

* **Support for learning**
  - learning in and out of school is seen as a coherent whole

* **Support for teaching**
  - parents are seen as partners in pupils' learning

* **Organisation and Communication**
  - parents...are informed about school policies and practice

* **Recognition of achievement**
  - awards rather than punishment is the prevailing approach throughout the school
  - there is consensus in the school about what is regarded as success

* **Home-School links**
  - parents play an active part in their children's learning
  - parents are confident that problems will be dealt with and feedback given
  - parent-teacher meetings are useful and productive
  - pupil progress is monitored and shared with parents on a regular basis

The authors wish to acknowledge the assistance of the National Union of Teachers in granting permission for the above headings and sub-headings featuring in 'Schools speak for themselves : Towards a framework for self-evaluation' (1996) to be reproduced here.

Partnership ... at a price

As Bastiani (1995) states, 'working with parents has shifted from being an optional activity, on the margins of school life, to a key task for all schools and all teachers' (10). It is generally acknowledged that partnership with parents is advantageous but this can only be achievable if there is a will to make a success of it on both sides. However, for the sake of the child, it is important that we reach all parents and not only the motivated ones.

While acknowledging the valuable contribution made by parents, in a paper the authors submitted to a conference entitled *Ruling the Margins: Problematising Parental Involvement* (Brito and Waller 1992b), we made the claim that it is unwise to treat them as having expertise equivalent to that of teachers. Unfortunately parents are not a homogeneous body, their viewpoints are diverse and unlikely to be unanimous. Bastiani (1992), contributing to the same conference, comments in a similar vein:

> Studies of actual parents, for example reveal the differences of ideology, expectation and experience that, at one and the same time, both reinforce and cut across differences of religion, race, class and culture ... from the perspective of, say, politicians or professionals, the more obvious reality is that parents 'speak with many voices!'

A curriculum negotiated between parents, teachers and children would prove totally impractical. Teachers would become the victims of lay pressure, possibly unable to make judgements which they believe to be in the child's best interest. As long as nearly fifteen years ago, the National Union of Teachers' report on *Home–School Relations and Adults in School* (1983) commented that

> the teacher's judgements are based on experiences of other children and age groups, as well as a professional training. They are focused on the particular child by the teacher's knowledge of that child's work and attitudes, refined as a result of discussions with colleagues, including the head, advisory staff and the child's parents. No adult other than the teaching staff will possess that amalgam of knowledge. (8)

Wikely (1986) and a colleague, running a series of parent–child workshop sessions, questioned whether parents and teachers actually speak the same language or whether a lot of assumptions are made on both sides that actually get in the way of communication.

Questionnaire evidence from Moordown's latest parental survey (1997) has revealed they are eager to understand more about the curriculum and about teaching methods, as well as receiving guidance on helping their child at home. As parents gain a clearer picture of the skills and efforts of the school they also become aware of its inefficiencies, and this knowledge places them in a position to be able to criticise ideas and practice. However, as the following parental extracts reveal, this generates a range of contradictory views, all of which will need to be addressed:

INTRODUCTORY PARENTS' EVENING
'... this was long and could have been shortened to around half an hour.'
'... the introductory evening was useful and informative.'

SCHOOL ETHOS
'... I'm very happy with the family atmosphere at this school.'
'... I feel that the school is considered elitist.'

DISCIPLINE/BEHAVIOUR
'... refreshingly high standard.'
'... there have been some recent behavioural problems.'

SCHOOL NEWSLETTER
'... excellent communication – full of information, ideas; fun and useful.'
'... too long, frequent and detailed ... a waste of paper and money.'

PARENTAL CONCERNS

'... we have concerns for the children with special needs. The school just encourages the able children.'

'... there is plenty of professional help for the less able but what facilities are there for the gifted children?'

We take comfort from the fact that the research of Atkin *et al.* (1988) highlighted similar problems to ours, namely that new developments can produce a new set of problems. As parents become more experienced at dealing with schools they can also become more vocal. Involving parents in the education process requires an extension of teachers' professionalism. Teachers are now having to educate not only children but also parents and other adults, and are often ill-equipped for this role.

In the main, the various partnership initiatives reported in this book have produced positive outcomes, most notably in the changing behaviour and attitudes of those involved. While children are able to observe the purposeful interaction between a parent and teacher, it may be that parents should have the right *to participate in but NOT dominate* the educational scene, *to influence but NOT control* curriculum practice, for opinions will never be unanimous. As Sallis (1997) wisely observes, 'true partnership will be achieved when parents and teachers come to value each others' skills and can work together within a framework of respect and mutual understanding' (16).

Parents now have opportunities for being involved in a multitude of ways, not simply baking cakes for the annual school fete. We have certainly come a long way since playground signs stated: 'Parents must not proceed beyond this point'!

Bibliography

Alexander, T., Beresford, E., Bastiani, J. (1995) *Home School Policies: Practical Guide*. Nottingham: JET Publications.

Ashton, F. (1982) 'Teacher education: a critical view of skills training', *British Journal of In-Service Education* **8**(3), 160–7.

Atkin, J. and Bastiani, J. with Goode, J. (1988) *Listening to Parents: An Approach to the Improvement of Home–School Relations*. Beckenham: Croom Helm.

Bailey, P., Dray, A., Waller, H. (1997) *Individual Learning Needs: The School's SEN Policy*, revised. Bournemouth: Moordown St John's CE Primary School.

Barber, M., Myers, K., Denning, G., Graham, J., Johnson, M. (1997) *School Performance and Extra-Curricular Provision*. London: Department for Education and Employment, Improving Schools Project.

Barrett, G. (1986) *Starting School: An AMMA Digest; a summary of the Report commissioned by AMMA from the Centre for Applied Research in Education at the School of Education, University of East Anglia in Norwich*. London: Assistant Masters' and Mistresses' Association (AMMA).

Bastiani, J. (1978) *Written Communication between Home and School*. Nottingham: University of Nottingham School of Education.

Bastiani, J. (1991) *Building Bridges: Parental Involvement in Schools*. Windsor: NFER Nelson.

Bastiani, J. (1992) "No-One Ever Said It Was Gonna Be Easy!" Some features of the problematic nature of home–school relations in the UK', in *Ruling the Margins: Problematising Parental Involvement*, conference report. London: University of North London (IMPACT Project) in association with the University of London Institute of Education.

Bastiani, J. (1995) *Taking a Few Risks*. London: The Royal Society for the Encouragement of Arts, Manufactures and Commerce (RSA).

Bastiani, J. (1996) *Home–School Contracts and Agreements: Opportunity or Threat?* London: RSA.

Beaucham, L. and Borys, A. (1981) 'A strategy for uncovering teacher professional development needs', *British Journal of In-Service Education* **8**(1), 19–21.

Berger, E. (1987) *Parents as Partners in Education: the School and Home working together*, 2nd edn. Columbus, Ohio: Merrill Publishing Company.

Blunkett, D. (1996) Letter to John Bastiani, reported in Bastiani, J. *Home–School Contracts and Agreements: Opportunity or Threat?*, 12. London: RSA.

Bowen, D. (1996) *Education Welfare Service Tries to Address the Needs of the Individual*, OHT master produced by Principal Education Welfare Officer. Dorset: Dorset County Council Education, Libraries and Arts Directorate.

Brito, J. (1991a) *An Analysis of a Starting School Profile*, unpublished paper. Portsmouth: University of Portsmouth School of Education.

Brito, J. (1991b) *Who Benefits from a More Detailed Knowledge of the Pre-School Child?*, unpublished practitioner-based enquiry essay for the BEd (Hons) degree, 1990/92. Portsmouth: University of Portsmouth School of Education.

Brito, J. (1992) *An Evaluation of the Provision of a Structured Pre-School Package, Evolved by the School and Requiring Active Parental Participation*, dissertation for the BEd (Hons) degree. Portsmouth: University of Portsmouth School of Education.

Brito, J. and Waller, H. (1992a) *Early Milestones*. Cambridge: Letterland™ Ltd.; Glasgow: HarperCollins Ltd.

Brito, J. and Waller, H. (1992b) 'Partnership – at a price?', in *Ruling the Margins: Problematising Parental Involvement*, conference report. London: University of North London (IMPACT Project) in association with the University of London Institute of Education.

Campaign for State Education (CASE). (1996) *Home–School Policies, Not Home–School Contracts*, CASE leaflet.

Caspari, I. (1974) 'Parents as co-therapists', *Forum for the Advancement of Educational Therapy* **2** (Supplement).

Cleverly, S. and Waller, H. (1994) 'Everybody's nightmare: the annual parents' meeting', *Dorset Governor* **17** (December), 18–19.

Cohen, L. and Manion, L. (1989) *Research Methods in Education*, 3rd edn. London: Routledge.

Copeland, I. (1994) 'The secondary school prospectus and the challenge of Special Educational Needs', *Educational Studies* **20**(2), 237–50.

Crix, B. and Ladbrooke, A. (1997) *School Audit Manual for Primary Schools: A Practical Guide to Self-Evaluation*. London: Pitman Publishing.

Cunningham, C. and Davis, H. (1985) *Working with Parents: Frameworks for Collaboration*. Milton Keynes: Open University Press.

Currie, L.-A. and Bowes, A. (1988) 'A head start to learning: involving parents of children just about to start school', *Support for Learning* **3**(4), 196–200.

Davie, R. (1985) 'Equalities and inequalities in working together for children, in partnership with parents: a contrast in stress', *Partnership Papers* **6**. London: National Children's Bureau.

Davies, E. (1988) 'PR – why bother?', *Management in Education* **2**(1), 34–6.

Department of Education and Science (1985) *Better Schools*, Cmnd. Paper 9469. London: Her Majesty's Stationery Office.

Department of Education and Science. (1991) *The Parent's Charter: You and Your Child's Education*. London: DES.

Department for Education (1994) *Code of Practice on the Identification and Assessment of Special Educational Needs*. London: The Stationery Office.

Department for Education (1994) *Special Educational Needs: a guide for parents*. London: DFE.

Department for Education and Employment. (1996) *Guidance on School Prospectuses and Governors' Annual Reports in Primary Schools*. London: DfEE.

Department for Education and Employment/Department of Health (1996) *Supporting Pupils with Medical Needs*. London: DfEE/DoH.

Devlin, T. and Knight, B. (1990) *Public Relations and Marketing for Schools*. Harlow: Longman.

Dorset County Council Education Department (1993) *Parent and Child Early Learning Pack (Themes)*. Dorchester: Dorset County Council Education, Libraries and Arts Directorate.

Dorset Governor Services. (1995) *Managing the Budget*, workshop Pack for use with governors, staff and/or parents. Dorchester: Dorset County Council Education, Libraries and Arts Directorate.

Duignan, P. and MacPherson, R. (1989) 'Educational leadership: an Australian project', *International School of Educational Management* **3**(1), 12–23.

Education (1992) 'Church primaries most effective schools' **179**(22), 29 May, 433.

Fish, J. (chair) (1985) *Educational Opportunities for All? Report of the Committee reviewing provision to meet special educational needs*, Chapter 13. London: Inner London Education Authority.

Furze, T. and Conrad, A . (1997), 'A review of parent partnership schemes', in Wolfendale, S. (ed). *Working with Parents of SEN Children after the Code of Practice*, 82–97. London: David Fulton Publishers.

Galloway, D. (1982) 'Learning from experience: a course for advisory teachers', *British Journal of In-Service Education* **7**(1), 70–6.

Gann, N. (1997) *Improving School Governance: How Better Governors make Better Schools*. London: Falmer Press.

Goddard, S. (1988) *Parental Contribution to the 1981 Act*, unpublished research paper; for details, contact Dorset County Psychological Service, The Old Rectory, Winterborne Monkton, Dorchester, Dorset DT2 9PS.

Goddard, S. and Waller, H. (1990) *My Child ... My Story: Guidelines to Writing a Parental Profile*. Dorchester: Dorset County Council Education, Libraries and Arts Directorate (copies obtainable, at cost, from Pupil and Parent Services).

Gray, L. (1991) *Marketing Education*. Buckingham: Open University Press.

Griffiths, A. and Hamilton, D. (1984) *Parent, Teacher, Child*. London: Methuen.

Hannon, P. (1992) 'Conditions of learning at home and in school', in *Ruling the Margins: Problematising Parental Involvement*, conference report. London: University of North London (IMPACT Project) in association with the University of London Institute of Education.

Hardie, B. (1991) *Marketing the Primary School: An Introduction for Teachers and Governors*. Plymouth: Northcote House Publishers Ltd.

Heale, P., Orlik, S., Watkins, M. (1993) *Improving Schools from Within: School Based INSET Programmes for Professional Development*. Harlow: Longman Group UK.

Hepworth, D. (1996) 'Promoting a positive image', *Managing Schools Today* **6**(1), September, 30–2.

Her Majesty's Stationery Office (1993) *Education Act 1993*. London: HMSO.

Hinton, S. (1989) 'Dimensions of parental involvement: easing the transfer from pre-school to primary', in Wolfendale, S. (ed.) *Parental Involvement: Developing Networks Between School, Home and Community*, 20–33. London: Cassell.

Jowett, S. and Baginsky, M. (1991) 'Parents and education: issues, options and strategies', *Education Research* **33**, 199–205.

Jowett, S., Baginsky, M. with McNeil, M. (1991) *Building Bridges: Parental Involvement in Schools*. Windsor: NFER Nelson.

Kirkman, S. (1989) 'Me first ...', *Times Educational Supplement* **3829** (17 November), 25.

Knight, P. (1992) 'Secondary schools in their own words: the image in school prospectuses', *Cambridge Journal of Education* **22**, 55–67.

Knowles, M. (1990) *The Adult Learner: A Neglected Species*, 2nd edn. Houston, Texas: Gulf Publishing Company.

Laar, B. (1997) *TES Guide to Surviving School Inspection*. Oxford: Butterworth-Heinemann.

Leedy, P. (1989) *Practical Research: Planning and Design*. Basingstoke: Macmillan.

Long, R. (1983) *Involving Parents in Early Childhood Education: Development of a School-focused In-Service Course for Teachers*, unpublished MEd dissertation. Sheffield: University of Sheffield School of Education.

MacBeath, J., Boyd, B., Rand, J., Bell, S. (1996) *Schools Speak for Themselves: Towards a Framework for Self-Evaluation*. London: National Union of Teachers, in association with the University of Strathclyde Quality in Education Centre.

Mallett, R. (1995) 'Parents: SEN policy and practice', *Schools' Special Educational Needs Policies Pack*, discussion papers IV, 7-12. London: National Children's Bureau.

Malthouse, I. (1995) *School Prospectuses Agreement Form*, proforma produced by the Information Officer, Professional Development Services. Dorset: Dorset County Council Education, Libraries and Arts Directorate.

Maxwell, E. and Hofkins, D. (1996) 'A mixed reception', *Times Educational Supplement* **4195** (22 November), 12.

Metherell, C. (1991) 'Space for marketing', *School Governor* (February/March), 20–1.

Merttens, R. (1992) 'A double-edged tool', *Times Educational Supplement*, **3986** (20 November), 16.

Meyerstein, C. (1992) 'Enlisting expertise', *Managing Schools Today* **1**(6), 38–40.

Morgan, R. (1986) *Helping Children Read – the Paired Reading Handbook*. London: Methuen.

Morgan, R. and Gavin, P. (1988) 'Paired reading: evaluation and progress', *Support for Learning* **3**(4), 201–6.

Mortimer, P., Sammons, P., Stoll, L., Lewis, D., Ecob, R. (1988) *School Matters: The Junior Years*. London: Open Books.

Mountfield, A. (1991) 'Marketing Morals', *Managing Schools Today* **1**(3), 26–7.

Narins, P. (1995a) 'Choosing the right administration method for your research', *Survey Sampling* **56**, 6–7.

Narins, P. (1995b) 'Guidelines for creating better questionnaires', *Survey Sampling* **58**, 8–9.

Narins, P. (1996) 'Get better info from all your questionnaires', *Survey Sampling* **59**, 8.

National Union of Teachers (1983) *Home–School Relations and Adults in School*. London: NUT.

Neal, R., Fuller, M., McPherson, H. (1990) *Junior Records of Achievement: Teacher's Guide*. Harlow: Longman Group UK Ltd.

Newton, C. and Tarrant, T. (1992) *Managing Change in Schools*. London: Routledge.

Office for Standards in Education (OFSTED) (1993) *Achieving Good Behaviour in Schools*. London: The Stationery Office.

Office for Standards in Education (OFSTED) (1995) *Homework in Primary and Secondary Schools*. London: The Stationery Office.

Office for Standards in Education (OFSTED) (1996) *The Implementation of the Code of Practice for Pupils with Special Educational Needs*. London: The Stationery Office.

The Oxford Large Print Dictionary (1995) 2nd. edn. ed. E. Pollard. Oxford: Oxford University Press.

Parnes, S. and Meadow, A. (1959) 'Effects of brainstorming instructions on creative problem-solving by trained and untrained subjects', *Journal of Educational Psychology* **50**, 171–6.

Petch, A. (1986) 'Parental choice at entry to primary school', *Research Papers in Education* **1**(1), 26–47.

Pope, A. (1980) 'The teacher as learner: some factors in the learning process', *British Journal of In-Service Education* **8**(3), 177–80.

PRIME (Primary Initiatives in Mathematical Education) (1987) *PRIME Newsletter* **3**. Cambridge: Homerton College PRIME Project.

Sallis, J. (1997) 'Partnerships not contracts', *Times Educational Supplement* **4235** (29 August), 16.

School Curriculum and Assessment Authority (1997) *Baseline Assessment Scales: Teacher's Guide*. London: SCAA.

Smith, H. (1975) *Strategies of Social Research: The Methodological Imagination*. London: Prentice/Hall International Inc.

Solity, J. and Raybould, E. (1988) *A Teacher's Guide to Special Needs: a Positive Response to the 1981 Education Act*. Milton Keynes: Open University Press.

Stacey, M. (1991) *Parents and Teachers Together*. Milton Keynes, Open University Press.

Sudman, S. and Bradburn, N. (1982) *Asking Questions: A Practical Guide to Questionnaire Design*. San Francisco, California: Jossey-Bass Inc.

Taylor Committee (1977) *A New Partnership for our Schools*. London: Department of Education and Science.

Tizard, B. and Hughes, M. (1984) *Young Children Learning: Talking and Thinking at Home and at School*. London: Fontana.

Tizard, B., Mortimore, J., Burchell, B. (1981) *Involving Parents in Nursery and Infant Schools: a Source Book for Teachers*. London: Grant McIntyre.

Topping, K. and Wolfendale, S. (eds) (1985) *Parental Involvement in Children's Reading*. London: Croom Helm.

Tulloch, M. (1997) 'The case against Home–school contracts', *Primary School Manager* (January/February), 23.

Walker, R. (1985) *Doing Research*. London: Routledge.

Waller, H. (1989) *The Parent/Professional Partnership in the Management of Individual Learning Needs*, unpublished dissertation for the Certificate of Advanced Professional Studies, 1988/89. Exmouth: Polytechnic South-West (now University of Plymouth), Rolle Faculty of Education.

Waller, H. (1992a) 'Asthma in schools: one school's approach', *Asthma Care Today* **1** (Summer), 37.

Waller, H. (1992b) 'Sharing expertise at Moordown St John's', in Wolfendale, S. *Empowering Parents and Teachers: Working for Children*, 148–56. London: Cassell.

Waller, H. (1993a) *The Production of a Small-Scale and Partial External Relations Audit of Moordown St John's CE Primary School, Bournemouth, Dorset*, essay submitted in partial fulfilment of the degree of MA(Ed). Southampton: University of Southampton Faculty of Educational Studies.

Waller, H. (1993b) 'Primary perceptions', *Managing Schools Today* **3**(1), September, 21–3.

Waller, H. (1993c) 'Asthma at school', *Head Teachers Review* (Winter), 16–18.

Waller, H. (1995) *Breath of Hope: the Management of Child Asthma in Primary Schools*, MA(Ed) dissertation. Southampton: University of Southampton Faculty of Educational Studies.

Waller, H. (1996) 'The management of child asthma in primary schools', *Asthma in General Practice* **4**(1), January, 12–13.

Waller, H., Johnston, P., Bellamy, D. (1992) *Asthma: True or False Game*. Bournemouth: Moordown St John's CE Primary School.

Wells, G. (1987) *The Meaning Makers: Children Learning Language and Using Language to Learn*. London: Hodder and Stoughton.

Wikely, F. (1986) 'Communication between parents and teachers', *Perspectives* **24**, 38–43. Exeter: University of Exeter School of Education.

Wolfendale, S. (1983) *Parental Participation in Children's Development and Education*. New York: Gordon and Breach.

Wolfendale, S. (1985a) 'Parental involvement in children's development and education: an overview', *Education and Child Psychology* **2**(1), 3–9.

Wolfendale, S. (1985b) 'Advice on your child (revised Guidelines)', in Wolfendale, S. (ed.) (1988) *The Parental Contribution to Assessment*, Developing Horizons in Special Education Series 10. NASEN (National Association of Special Educational Needs): NASEN House, 4/5 Amber Business Village, Amber Close, Tamworth, Staffs B77 4RP. (Also in several other books.)

Wolfendale, S. (1987) 'The evaluation and revision of "All About Me"', *Early Child Development and Care* **29**, 473–558.

Wolfendale, S. (1988) *The Parental Contribution to Assessment*, Developing Horizons in Special Education Series 10. NASEN (National Association of Special Educational Needs), NASEN House, 4/5 Amber Business Village, Amber Close, Tamworth, Staffs B77 4RP.

Wolfendale, S. (ed.) (1989) *Parental Involvement: Developing Networks Between School, Home and Community*. London: Cassell.

Wolfendale, S. (1990) *All About Me*. Nottingham: NES/Arnold.

Wolfendale, S. (1992a) *Empowering Parents and Teachers: Working for Children*. London: Cassell.

Wolfendale, S. (1992b) *Primary Schools and Special Needs: Policy, Planning and Provision*, 2nd. edn. London: Cassell.

Wolfendale, S. (1993a), 'Involving parents in assessment', in Wolfendale, S. (ed.) *Assessing Special Educational Needs*, 150–65. London: Cassell.

Wolfendale, S. (1993b) *Baseline Assessment: a Review of Current Practice, Issues and Strategies for Effective Implementation*, OMEP(UK) Report. Stoke-on-Trent: Trentham Books.

Wolfendale, S. (1995) 'Parental involvement', *Schools' Special Educational Needs Policies Pack*, Discussion papers IV, 15–21. London: National Children's Bureau.

Wolfendale, S. (ed.) (1997a) *Working with Parents of SEN Children after the Code of Practice*. London: David Fulton Publishers.

Wolfendale, S. (1997b) *Department for Education and Employment (DfEE) commissioned research into the GEST-funded 'Parent Partnership Scheme'*. London: DfEE.

Youngman, M. (1978) *Designing and Analysing Questionnaires*. Rediguide 12. Nottingham: University of Nottingham School of Education.

Index